NATIONAL INFORMATION RESOURCES FOR SOCIAL SCIENCES IN INDIA

CONCEPTS IN COMMUNICATION
INFORMATICS & LIBRARIANSHIP
(CICIL)

For a list of titles in this series,
see pp. 189-92 at the end of the book

ABOUT THE AUTHOR

S.P. Agrawal (*b.* 1929) was Director, National Social Science Documentation Centre, ICSSR, and Member Secretary, Indian Association of Social Science Institutions. He was also the Vice-Chairman of the Asia and Pacific Information Network in Social Sciences (APINESS). In 1988 he was awarded the degree of Doctor of Philosophy in Education (honoris causa) by International University Foundation. Presently, he is Member, Round Table on Research in Reading, IFLA, and Member, International Committee for Social Science Information and Documentation. He is also Member of Board of Archival Studies, National Archives of India, and Hindi Advisory Committee, Ministry of Coal, Government of India. He has written extensively on various aspects of education as well as of library and information science.

Concepts in Communication
Informatics & Librarianship-36

National Information Resources for Social Sciences in India

Mobilisation, Dispersal and International Enhancement

S.P. AGRAWAL
Former Director
National Social Science Documentation Centre, ICSSR, New Delhi

CONCEPT PUBLISHING COMPANY, NEW DELHI 110059

ISBN 81-7022-429-2

First Published 1992

Published and Printed by
Ashok Kumar Mittal
Concept Publishing Company
A/15-16, Commercial Block, Mohan Garden
NEW DELHI-110059 (India)

Lasertypeset by
Microtech Advance Printing Systems (Pvt.) Ltd.
H-13, Bali Nagar
NEW DELHI-110015

GENERAL EDITOR'S INTRODUCTION

Although the developing countries have enormous manpower at their disposal, they lack resources to utilise this asset to full advantage. What we need today for speedy development in every field of our activity is to harness manpower productively through effective application of information technology. One of the key factors for phenomenal development of Science and Technology in the West was that the scientists there had long back realised the value and importance of information resources in their research and development activities. The information dissemination made at the right time and in rightly adequate measure can do wonders. It will be truism to say that no other technology has had such an impact as information technology on the way we live and the manner we work. It can enrich an individual's life, can prove an effective instrument in increasing the competency of a government agency and the productivity of a business enterprise.

Developed societies are far ahead of developing countries in the application of information technology. The latter will have to make a long march to catch up with the Western countries for proper and optimum utilisation of information resources. India too lags behind in this regard; but the record is not too dismal. Appreciable progress has been made in the utilisation of this vital resource in the domain of Science and Technology in the post-Independence period. However, the recognition of the importance of information science in the management of Social Science resources has come very late. As a matter of fact, it was only in 1969 with the establishment of Indian Council of Social Science Research as an autonomous body fully funded by the Government of India, which opened up a new era in the development of the Social Sciences. The creation of the erstwhile Documentation Wing of the Council turned into Social Science Documentation Centre (SSDC) and now National Social Science Documentation Centre (NASSDOC) was a step in the right direction and undoubtedly within two decades of its existence NASSDOC changed the scenario of documentation in Social Sciences

The contribution of the library profession in developing information science can hardly be over-emphasised. It does not make much of a difference that Information Science has been developed through the application of electronics to data manipulation or that it is the latest version of librarianship. The main point is that both the automation and the librarianship have played their part in its present development — complementary to each other. Tracing the history of the Information Science, we find its close relationship with librarianship. Librarians who were engaged in catering to the needs of the scientific community were constantly under pressure to obtain the services of the computer to handle incessant flow of scientific data for use.

The present book in CICIL series presents a detailed picture of the national information resources in Social Sciences in India. The resources have been categorised into (i) Content (Specialised) resources which include Indian Periodicals, Dissertations and Government Publications, (ii) Human resources, and (iii) Institutional resources. In the context of human resources, extensive linking of would-be professionals with those at decision-making level to produce better results in the mobilisation of information resources is strongly pleaded. The reason for this is not far to seek. *Administrators are generally too pre-occupied to pay heed to what human resources development concepts entail. Even intellectuals and professionals, when they happen to be at the decision-making level, neglect, rather tend to dismantle, whatsoever infrastructure is there, just for the sake of immediate short-term benefits and administrative convenience; and this, despite sufficient realisation that decision-making should be done on the basis of proven result.*

A notable feature of the book is that it makes out a case for setting up three apex national bodies, which would make every endeavour to co-ordinate the activities and obtain the co-operation of individual information centres within a determined framework. They will strive to improve the information services and standardise the information technology and methods for smooth working of the interchange of information. Introduction of automation in some selective institutions will also be one of their responsibilities. The book spells out in detail what the aims and objectives of these bodies should be, how they will function and what pivotal role National Social Science Documentation Centre could play in helping them to function effectively and efficiently so as to achieve their desired goals. The book also proposes a scheme of document supply service for the Capital City of Delhi, where a large cluster of libraries of different types exists. Though the task is daunting, the scheme can be effectively implemented if the library profession extends its full co-operation. If it makes a success, it will undoubtedly prove a great boon to both the librarians and the information seekers, and can also be introduced in other metropolitan cities of India.

A note of caution: Of necessity, there is duplication of fact and ideas in various chapters.

S.P. AGRAWAL

CONTENTS

PART IV
Linkages

APPENDICES

PART I

INTRODUCTORY ANALYSIS

1

SOCIAL SCIENCE INFORMATION RESOURCES AND THEIR DISPERSAL IN DEVELOPING COUNTRIES: Indian Experience

While we may not agree in toto about the subjects to be included in social sciences, I think we understand what is meant by underdeveloped/developing countries.

Most of them have not had the good fortune of possessing good information resources, and in the case of a few who do, they appear to suffer from lack of organisation and coordination.

Information resources, as we know, comprise macro-documents, micro-documents, grey material, unconventional material, etc., and also knowledge experts. We in India also include *time* element as a resource. Developing countries have first of all to organise them properly to make them useful to potential users.

If one feels tempted to say that developed countries are way ahead and they have already taken steps to document resources and make them available on demand with the help of modern technology, we must remind ourselves that the services in developing countries are not free and they can ill afford to seek this easy way out.

The problem that we are seized with primarily depends on economic resources for their solution. I suspect that constraints will always be there even in the best of circumstances. A solution to get over this situation is resource sharing and networking—but then that too requires budget. And when it comes to allocating scarce economic resources, the balance is more likely to tilt in favour of other sciences, other activities. By nature perhaps powers that be, tend to allocate morbidly more for defence—fight against man rather than that against hunger. And, therefore, social science information is an item of low priority obviously for governments. There is no point bemoaning over this.

We are in the midst of an information explosion in developing countries with the continuous accumulation of information and its proliferation at a tremendous rate. The computer technology has helped us to bring a lot of information resources under bibliographical control. Much information resources are still out of our reach in developing countries, like in-house reports of organizations, conference proceedings, research project reports, government reports, R & D results, etc.

In our sector of the world, that is, in developing countries, the greatest challenge faced by information centres is to provide information to the user which is accurate, timely and systematic. Information overload, however, is as much dangerous as is insufficient or wrong-fed information. Our information centres are on the right track, but they must continue to move forward while they sift, evaluate and synthesize information before serving them to users.

Peter Lazar holds the view that information resources including information systems and networks can only be effectively used by a country if adequate national information infrastructures have been built. And without an infrastructure and machinery to handle information and to make it accessible within the country in the form required by the different user groups, no country can benefit by the efforts made by developed countries as also international organisations to help channelling the necessary information at the right moment to users. In fact, it is our Indian experience that this deadens national information resources. This is not to say that technical assistance, guidelines for information policy, planning and management from all these sources is not welcome. I recall Makaminan Makagiansar's observations during launch of APINESS in May 1986. And I quote:

> "Information, understood as communicable form of knowledge, is a big ocean; we need proper navigating devices to wade through it, and to dip into it in search of needed pearls of wisdom."

Still, it is again our experience in India that just as navigating sophisticated devices developed by affluent owners cannot be used by boatmen of Kerala coast in India, no national information infrastructure is going to work if it is not based on sound national information policy—and I repeat *national information policy*.

Sam Pitroda, the then Adviser to Prime Minister on Technology

Missions in India, in his address to International Conference on Bibliographic Data Bases and Networks, (February, 1989) emphasised that the merger of communication and computer technologies had given an impetus to the whole new thinking in organising, structuring, transmitting and manipulating information to derive a variety of outputs. No other technology has had such an impact as information technology on the way we live and the way we work. The importance of linking information and the people to harness the power of information to meet the basic needs of the people, can hardly be overemphasised. An adjustment to the new work environment, work culture and work standards, is called for. And most importantly, manpower, India's biggest asset, must be utilised most productively.

The adequate or at least satisfactory use of information sources in developing countries should not elude us if we keep in mind that:

We, in the developing countries, have much lagged behind in *application of information technology*. And as such, if the researchers have personal computers on their working tables and public funds to squander, they will like to have interactive facilities with databases situated thousands and thousands of miles away in some developed country, ignoring the national information sources, which are not available on-line. As Yogesh Atal put it during APINESS meeting, out of about 900 bibliographical and numerical data bases now available on-line internationally, only about three quarter of a per cent are to be found in developing countries, and because of the poor organisation of information in the third world, it is out of reach of the general user.

Information management programme is still a low priority area in the developmental schemes of developing countries. As a result there is poor management of information resources. In India, leaving aside agricultural field where satisfactory achievement has been accomplished in transferring information from lab to field, most of the other information generated, does not reach the actual users.

Lack of *information dissemination channels*, results in a situation like the one, where, Railway Board of India, at one time did not know about availability of indigenous technology for railway computerisation programme at a much lower cost than the recommended foreign technology of 1300 crores.

There is general lack of *information consciousness*. The scientists, researchers and academicians in the developing countries generally accord a low priority to information conservation. The information centres providing access to these information resources are considered useful but not essential. Information as a usable resource is not considered important by information generators, and therefore, no conscious effort is made to preserve and make it available to others. This results in poor utilisation of whatever information infrastructure is available.

As Tamas Foldi in his study of social science information and social practice has urged, the "dispersed and non-transparent structure of data and their storage delineate demand on data and efficiency of use", and a mission oriented and multidisciplinary approach manifesting itself in service of synthetic nature and direct and steady access by the user to the data base are required.

In any case, the cumulative effect has been the neglect of our information resources and data bases and increasing dependence on the information resource and data bases in the developed countries, meaning thereby that our information resources are not adequately used, whereas the information data bases of developed countries, already adequately used, are also in demand in developing countries.

Quite obviously, developing countries will have to gear efforts towards adequate dissemination of information about their own information resources, which alone can bear fruits.

And for this, the minimum that needs to be done is: (i) to enhance user friendliness of information system, (ii) to cooperate in order to be able to offer a great variety of types of information, and to specialise in serving specific user groups, and (iii) to ameliorate retrieval system so as to reduce unspecific and redundant information.

Information is like any other tradeable commodity and we require to sell it through proper distribution channels for effective and adequate returns, just as we have so far sold information carriers (i.e., books, etc.).

It is obvious that no information centre can be self-sufficient as far as the collection development of information is concerned, because (i) there are limited funds, and (ii) all information sources are not available for purchase. Therefore, in order to improve services, information centres must be interdependent to support one another. It is not the size of collection but accessibility by which quality of information centres is measured. It would also mean that what is not used in one particular information centre will be available for adequate use in some other information centre if both are participating in resource sharing cooperation programme. It is, however, not so simple as it may seem, and Jean Meyriat, as far back as 1960, cautioned:

> "The very nature of the information in question—the fact that it concerns the social sciences—creates a number of obstacles to cooperation, which it is important to identify, if we were to seek more effective means of overcoming them".

Cost analysis has two parameters. One is the expenditure incurred on a particular unit of activity, and the other relates to the value one has to pay to acquire it. Tamas Foldi had, in a presentation before FID/SD meeting in September 1984, interpreted the concepts of the information market:

> "It is in the interest of the society that a considerable part of information be generally accessible. The cost of information production is, therefore, partly covered by society, and a particularly great role is played by society (the state, public bodies, non-profit institutions) in covering cost of access to information" and that "because of its economic nature, information is a special type of commodity. Production costs cannot be fully returned, nor can property rights be effectively defended for all types of information".

Some other scholars like Raju M. Methew opine that the value of information as a resource or market commodity for a particular country or society depends on the level of information literacy or awareness of that particular country or society. In an information literate society, information is a scarce resource which is valued highly and used accordingly. In an information illiterate society there is little possibility of handing it in an effective manner, and therefore, the value of information is negligible. It is only when a society attains information literacy, it starts to generate, collect, process and utilize high level information in an effective way and comparatively at less costs.

If that be so—and our Indian experience indicates it is —the cost factor has to be viewed accordingly if only to be able to stand alive in this *information explosion*—and we could as well add *misinformation explosion, disinformation explosion*.

For adequate utilization of information, we have to identify users, In fact, not users in general but "one who has a need". According to Maurice B. Line there is no word that means "one who has a need". But why I say this is because 'users', i.e., those who use are expected to know what they had used and where they got it. The problem of inadequate utilisation of the commodity will generally not arise then. But in the case of "one who has a need" and does not know where to get it, the information source will remain un-utilized.

With the dissemination of knowledge and expansion of individual education, the categories of those "who have a need" are an ever-increasing process. Normally, there are two broad categories. Individual researchers, practitioners and project teams constitute one group. Their interests generally lie in research in progress. Policy-makers, planners, and decision-makers for RD endeavour fall in the other category. They need to know about research trends, thrust areas, gaps, fallow region requiring cultivation and duplication of efforts to eliminate it, etc.

Tamas Foldi had divided users of economic information according to their fields of activities in (i) Economic research and education, (2) Economic policy-making, and (3) Economic activity. In further division Foldi distinguishes among (1) decision-makers, (2) those preparing decisions, and (3) practising of operative economists. Combing these clusters comes to nine groups with different economic needs. I tend to agree with H.P. Hogeweg de Hart that this classification is equally applicable to users in all social science disciplines and/or social sciences as a whole.

Their identification, in a way, will not be so difficult a task, if we do what 'sellers' do. 'display'—Display what we have and 'window shopping', as it is called, will attract different categories to different items, giving us ample opportunity to identify.

All said and done, we have to acknowledge that developing countries have also maintained the pace of development of information technology covering the entire range from collection, storage, processing, dissemination and use of available information by the user notwithstanding that, in the nineties, information centres in developing countries will have to face a big challenge. On the one hand, the resource crunch will make it obligatory for information centres to economise, standardize procedures, reduce staffing levels to make more efficient use of existing facilities. On the other, information centres will be required to offer a wider range of user services as well as enhanced administrative and intellectual control over information.

In India, this is how we started. First of all the Planning Commission mooted the idea of setting up Indian Council of Social Science Research (ICSSR). Under it, in turn, was founded the documentation wing in 1970.

It started and completed a massive project of Union Catalogue of Social Science Serials and Periodicals. Lists of Professional Organisations and Research Institutions were prepared. Later, National Register of Social Scientists was also compiled.

In the year 1973, the then Education Minister of Government of India Professor Nurul Hasan, inaugurated the Inter-Library Resources Centre, which brought together holdings of research value from 38 local libraries under one roof.

India being a multilingual nation, the ICSSR Documentation Wing—National Social Science Documentation Centre (NASSDOC), as it is now called — is bringing out area and language bibliographies, prepares special subject bibliographies on request and also encourages other activities of this nature by extending financial aid.

The Centre provides travel grants to outstation scholars to come and consult material in Delhi and with the courier van it makes use of inter-library loan system for the sake of scholars to save them their time and energy, and also offers easy reproduction facility.

Abstracting journals, indexing journals, current contents, review publications, lists of research completed and in progress, translation services, personal information services, are put to use. Participation in Regional Networks like APINESS, and international cooperation as input centres has been taken up. All this and much more including dependable data banks, direct access of computer-stored information, fascimile transmission, etc., are on required to be put on the planning board.

It is only an aerial survey. It is not a substitute for an intensive study presentation. But nonetheless, it is an essential preliminary.

PART II

ABSTRACT

2

MOBILIZATION OF NATIONAL INFORMATION RESOURCES FOR THE SOCIAL SCIENCES IN INDIA AND THEIR INTERNATIONAL ENHANCEMENT

Proem

The merit and worth of our contribution to the needs of international community is in direct relation to the effective, efficient mobilization of our national resources.

It will not be unwise, therefore, to do some introspection and take stock of things. Over the years, we have prepared good schemes full of good ideas, and launched new projects with good intentions. However, somewhere along the line, our interest started to flag and instead of showing further progress, some stagnation or even sliding downwards is visible.

This is not a cry of despair but a note of caution so that we are geared to make the best use of new innovations for proper coordination of our resources along horizontal and vertical lines.

RESOURCES AVAILABLE IN INDIA

Primary Sources

PRINTED

Books: Books are the main source of primary information for the social scientist. According to a rough estimate, libraries of about 400 social science research institutes, besides university and government libraries, specialising in specific disciplines have been functioning in the country. Most of these have specialised collection of books which can be fruitfully exploited by the researchers. A discipline-wise select list of research institutes/information centres is given in Appendix-I.

Periodicals: Periodical literature is the most sought after material after books (in fact sometimes more than books). The specialised information centres (Appendix-II) maintain a good collection of current periodical literature. Most of these centres subscribe to about 200 current periodical titles on an average. At present the number of current Social Science titles published in India is about 2300, i.e., 43.4 per cent out of about 5300 titles published in all disciplines. National Social Science Documentation Centre (NASSDOC), New Delhi, as a policy, sub-scribes to all the worthwhile Social Science periodicals of research value published in India and selected number of journals in library and information science. It currently receives more than 3000 titles. The subscription is made for 500 journals and 22 newspapers, 2598 are received in exchange and rest against publication grant or gratis. The rate of Indian and foreign journals is 1:1. In the retrieval of old material, Interlibrary Resources Centre (ILRC), with a collection of about 1,00,000 volumes, has been playing an important role.

Newspapers: Newspapers, being the primary sources for official notifications/orders, policy matters, market information, import/ export data, etc., are also an important source of research material particularly for political scientists and economists.

Sometimes the most important research findings are first reported in newspapers. Some newspaper offices maintain back files of their papers and supply the old issues or photocopies on payment. On account of their large size, few research libraries/information centres maintain complete back files of the papers. Microform have now, however, made it possible to keep record of this rich resource within minimum available space. On a survey of holdings of newspapers in Delhi libraries, it has been observed that Jawaharlal Nehru University Library (New Delhi), including its Centre for Russian Studies has a good collection of newspapers published in Asian countries and Russia. Delhi University Library (Delhi) and Nehru Memorial Museum and Library (New Delhi) have collections of African and Indian newspapers respectively. Other notable libraries having useful collections are Central Secretariat Library, Ministry of External Affairs Library, Parliament Library, Indian Council of World Affairs Library (Press clipping), etc. The general trend is towards discarding hard copy files in favour of microcopies. NASSDOC has an approved programme of acquiring microcopies of the back files of newspapers which are not available in libraries in Delhi.

Government Publications: Socio-economic surveys, national development programmes/plans, progress reports of the Ministries/ Departments, and statistical data documents form an important part of the Government publications. In Delhi, Central Secretariat Library, Parliament Library, Ministry of External Affairs Library, Ministry of Home Affairs Library, Planning Commission Library, etc., maintain good collection not only of Central and State Government publications but also of the publications of the foreign governments.

Statistical Data: It has been observed that statistical data is used more by social scientists than by others. A large volume of data is available with the Government departments, research institutions, university departments and individuals but there are no worthwhile centralised statistical data centres to store data generated at different places and make it available to researchers.

Partial attempts are being made in this direction by some organisations. ICSSR Data Archives (New Delhi) maintains data from out of the research reports financed by ICSSR. The Small Industries Extension Training Institute (Hyderabad) holds large data in the field of small industries. The Small Industrial Development Organisation (Delhi) also maintains data in the same field.

According to the status report (1983) National Informations Centre (New Delhi) has developed statistical data bases at district headquarters in each of the 26 States in India, to meet Governmental needs.

GREY SOURCES

Research Reports: These form an important segment of monographs consulted by researchers. NASSDOC is perhaps the biggest collection centre for the reports in India. It receives copies of reports from the institutions and individual scholars under contractual obligation to ICSSR for its providing financial assistance and also as a result of its extensive exchange of publications programme, operative not only in the country but also abroad. It has at present a collection of about 2000 research reports.

Theses: Of special significance to researchers in social sciences is the collection of unpublished PhD. theses. Each university library keeps and maintains a record of the theses approved by the university. NASSDOC, at present however, is the biggest thesis collecting centre in the country. It acquires a copy of the thesis from the scholars on a token payment of Rs. 400. The total collection at present is about 2500.

Working Papers: A large number of working papers (mostly typed scripts) are brought out in India. Indian Council of Social Science Research (New Delhi), which has been set up to coordinate research programmes in India, receives copies of most of the working papers released by these institutes/centres financed by the Government.

Manuscripts: Manuscripts are mostly consulted by the historians. India's cultural tradition goes back to the hoary past. The glimpses of our glorious heritage and its social surroundings can still be had from the old manuscripts available in the country's archives. Some of the notable resources centres keeping record of such material are:

1. Bhandarkar Oriental Research Institute, Pune;
2. Government Oriental Manuscript Library, Madras;
3. Khuda Baksh Oriental Public Library, Patna;
4. National Archives of India, New Delhi;
5. National Library, Calcutta; and
6. Raza Library, Rampur.

NON-CONVENTIONAL SOURCES

Physical formats: Microforms, Video-cassettes, Floppy discs, Tapes, etc. Hard copies form the major part of the backfiles collection in information centres. But to cope with the space problem, backfiles of journals, PhD. theses, research project reports, publications like annual report, newsletter, brochures, etc., are now preferred to be maintained in microform. Some of the titles in this format available in NASSDOC are:

1. *Annals of Indian Administration*;
2. *Anthropological Society of Bombay Journal*;
3. *Bombay Geographical Society Journal*;
4. *Economic Working Papers (U.K.)*;
5. *Gujarat Research Society Journal*;
6. *Indian Linguistics*;
7. *Psychological Abstracts*;

8. *Social Action*;
9. *A Bibliography of Mughal India, 1526-1707*, by R.A. Sharma;
10. *Castes and Tribes of Southern India*, by E. Thurston and K. Ramachari (7 vols); and
11. *NASSDOC Research Information Series*.

Beginning has also been made in the acquisition of documents in machine readable form, i.e., Floppy discs, Tapes. Some of the publications available in this format in NASSDOC are:

1. *Economic and Political Weekly Index*;
2. *India 2000: An Annotated Bibliography*;
3. *List of Current Periodicals in NASSDOC*; and
4. *Core List of Social Science Periodicals*.

Secondary Sources

The role of secondary sources is to help introduce the right source of information to the user. There are different forms of it compiled at national and international level. The emphasis here is on Indian compilations because these cover the maximum volume of national material needed most by the scholars. Notable among these sources are:

1. Specialised current indexing and abstracting services including SDI;
2. Retrospective indexes;
3. Bibliographies;
4. Union Catalogues; and
5. Technical and Socio-Economic Information Indicators.

Almost all the information and documentation centres generate/ acquire, maintain and service these sources.

MOBILISATION OF RESOURCES

Historical Perspective

Indian way of life has always attached greatest importance to the development, mobilisation and dissemination of knowledge in all walks of life. We are inheritors of a tradition where knowledge has come down to us through more than 3000 years. The Vedas, for instance, have been passed from generation to generation through oral tradition known as *Shruti* and *Smriti*, i.e., to listen and to retain. Perhaps the outstanding mobilization of information resources in ancient India was the *Bhrigu Samhita* which records almost all human activities in the form of analysis of birth charts. Side by side, we had also the tradition of preserving manuscripts, mainly palmleaf at places called *Bharati Bhandars* and *Saraswati Bhandars*, which were usually attached to temples. A work of King Trillokyamalle, a Western Chalukyan ruler, refers to custodians (i.e., librarians) of these store houses of information sources as *Saraswati Bhandarikas*. This tradition continued during Middle Ages. The libraries attached to *dargahs* (tombs/shrines), *madrasas* (schools) and mosques were suitably maintained. (Mohammed Taher, et al, 1986, Dargah Libraries in India: A Comparative Study, *International Library Review*, 18, 1986, p 337-45). Thus mobilization of information resources in the sense of collecting and preserving books, manuscripts, information source in the form of oral (folk literature) and/or written work, that is, books and manuscrips has existed in India from times immemorial, and in the early part of 10th century it began to be treated as a distinct activity of specialisation with its own normative principles, techniques, theories and practices.

Mobilization of resources, as we understand today, came to India to serve the British administration. Ethnographic surveys formed an important feature in the decennial Census operations in India and in the publication of several provincial Gazetteers. A large corpus of data, gathered uninterrupted for over a century, are published in the Census reports and handbooks. These publications constitute a vast source of data on anthropological details of all kinds in respect of the land and its people. The first Census was taken between 1865 and 1872, the second in 1881, and thereafter every ten years. The last Census of India was taken in 1991. Thanks again to the painstaking efforts of British administrators, we have the district handbooks, a series of monographs on castes and tribes in India, and so on. Christian Missionaries, travellers and a few others also collected data on tribal and rural people and wrote about their life and culture in the *Journal of Asiatic Society of Bengal* (1784), *Indian Antiquary* (1872), *Journal of Anthropological Society of Bombay* (1886), *Mythic Society*

Quarterly Journal (1909), *Journal of Bihar and Orissa Research Society* (1915) and *Man in India* (1921), etc.

Mobilization of information resources alongside social science research in India got great impetus after Independence as a result of the socio-economic development process and the setting up of the Planning Commission by Government of India.

A real breakthrough came with the establishment of Indian Council of Social Science Research (ICSSR) in 1969 April as an autonomous body, which has made a signal contribution to the literature survey in social sciences by starting a series of titles devoted to different disciplines (Appendix-V).

So far as the Libraries and Information Centres are concerned, their development has also been very significant. In comparison to 1,000 libraries and information centres attached to scientific establishments, there are around 700 social science information centres and libraries attached to universities, government departments, research institutes and commercial organisations. Of course, all of these do not undertake documentation activities but most of the specialised ones do. Some of the important libraries of Institutions with their specialised field are mentioned in Appendix-II. All the University libraries (180); Indian Institute(s) of Technology; public libraries, like Khuda Baksh Oriental Public Library (Patna), National Library (Calcutta), and Government departmental libraries have a sizeable collection of source material on Social Sciences and generate information resources.

Besides these, information centres primarily engaged in documentation and mobilisation activities are: Centre on Rural Documentation, Hyderabad (1985); ICSSR Data Archives, New Delhi (1973); National Documentation Centre on Mass Communication, New Delhi (1976), National Institute for Educational Planning and Administration, New Delhi (1962); National Social Science Documentation Centre, New Delhi (1970).

The University Grants Commission, New Delhi after setting up Science Information Centre at Bangalore, has also set up Social Science Information Centres at SNDT University, Bombay and M.S. University, Baroda and plans to develop some more at other universities.

MOBILISATION ACTIVITIES

Bibliographical Control

PRINTED MATERIAL

Books: There is satisfactory bibliographical control of published literature. Some of the important tools are:

1. *Indian National Bibliography* (Central Reference Library, Calcutta), Monthly.
   Covers official and non-official material in English and regional languages in India.
2. *Accession List: South Asia* (U.S. Library of Congress Office, New Delhi), Monthly.
   Covers serial and non-serial material published in India and acquired for U.S. Library of Congress and other research libraries in U.S. participating in one or more country programmes.
3. *Catalogue of Government of India Civil Publications* (Controller of Publications, Delhi), Irregular.
4. *Indian Publisher*, *Indian Book Index*, *Indian Book Industry*, *Indian Book Review Index* and *Indian Book Chronicle* are also publications of this nature.
5. Lists of publications released by Government departments, Commissions and Study Teams are also helpful.
6. *Indian Books in Print*, *Reference Catalogue of Indian Books in Print* and *National Bibliography of Indian Literature* are important sources for retrospective researches.

Periodicals and Newspapers

1. *Press in India* (Registrar of Newspapers, New Delhi), Annual.
   Covers English and regional languages of India.
2. *Directory of Periodicals Published in India: A Classified Guide, 1986-87*, Sushil Kumar, New Delhi.

GREY MATERIAL

Doctoral Research: Of special significance to researchers in Social

Science is the collection of unpublished PhD. theses. Some of the tools for the identification of doctoral research are listed in Appendix-IV.

Non-doctoral Research: To avoid duplication and for judicious utilization of resources, setting up of data bases and proper bibliographical tools for search is absolutely necessary. Some of the tools are mentioned below:

1. *Census of Social Science Research in Southern States* (Madras Institute of Development Studies, Madras), Annual.
2. *Research Project Reports in NASSDOC: An Annotated Bibliography* (NASSDOC, New Delhi), Irregular.
   Covers titles acquired up to 1980.
3. *Social Science Research Index* (NASSDOC, New Delhi), Irregular.
4. *Catalogue of Government of India Civil Publications* (Controller of Publications, Delhi). Irregular.
   Lists researches conducted in Government departments and released in form of reports and surveys.
5. *ICSSR Newsletter* (ICSSR, New Delhi), Half Yearly.
   Includes information regarding ICSSR supported Research projects.
6. *ICSSR Research Projects, 1969-87* (ICSSR, New Delhi). Adhoc.

Manuscripts

The Ministry of Human Resource Development, Government of India, is considering the setting up of a Central Microfilm Library and Documentation Centre to locate, preserve and mobilize judicious use of rare manuscripts in the country. The Ministry already has a programme of providing financial assistance to the institutions for converting old documents into microfilm.

DISCIPLINE-ORIENTED BIBLIOGRAPHIES

A few selective bibliographies are:

1. *Annotated and Classified Bibliography of Indian Demography*

(ICSSR, New Delhi).

2. *Annotated Bibliography on the Economic History of India, A.D. 1500–A.D. 1947* (Gokhale Institute of Politics and Economic, Pune). 4 vols.
3. *Mahatma Gandhi Bibliography* (ICSSR, New Delhi). Bibliographies of writings on Gandhiji in Bengali, English, Hindi, Sanskrit and Urdu have so far been published.
4. *Asian Social Science Bibliography* (Institute of Economic Growth, New Delhi). (Since suspended).
5. *Jawaharlal Nehru: A Bibliography* (Vikas, New Delhi)
6. *Urban Studies in India: A Bibliography* (National Institute of Urban Affairs, 1988)
7. *Bibliography on Women at Work in India* (Institute of Social Studies, New Delhi)

Area Studies Bibliographies

Started in 1979 by NASSDOC cover literature on Indian States. So far information about 10,000 titles in English and Indian regional languages has been collected. The bibliography already released are:

1. Andaman and Nicobar Islands
2. Andhra Pradesh
3. Goa, Daman and Diu
4. Madhya Pradesh
5. Punjab, Haryana and Himachal Pradesh
6. Rajasthan

Language Bibliographies

Started in 1979 by NASSDOC cover research material in all disciplines in social sciences in English and Indian regional languages published in India. So far bibliographical data of about 6000 titles in Hindi, 2000 in Gujarati and 300 each in Kannada and Oriya languages has been collected.

Bibliographies on Demand

Select bibliographies on the topic of their research is the prime need of the scholars. More often this demand is met by the institutions where they work. But many of the libraries do not have the facility to provide this service. NASSDOC undertakes this service and receives on an average 600 requests annually from scholars and institutions all over India. The bibliographies compiled are reported in *ICSSR Newsletter*, NASSDOC's *Bibliographies on Tap*; *Bibliographic Reprints*; and cumulative listing made in the document, *Bibliography of Bibliographies*. The photocopies of these bibliographies are also made available on demand.

National Library (Calcutta), Indian Association of Special Libraries and Information Centres (Calcutta) and Association of Indian University (New Delhi) also provide this service on national level.

Important bibliographies compiled by these institutions are reported in *IASLIC Newsletter*.

Current Indexes

Indexing

Most of the discipline-oriented information centres bring out current awareness/documentation lists to keep their clientele informed about the latest literature. Some important tools generated for covering current and restrospective material are mentioned in Appendix-III. Besides these, National Council of Educational Research and Training, (New Delhi) and Indian Institute of Management (Ahmedabad) also include abstracts and reviews in their journals, *Indian Educational Review* and *Vikalpa* in the field of Education and Management respectively.

Retrospective Indexes

Indian Education Index (1947-1978), *Index to Indian Periodicals in Sociology and Psychology* (1886-1970) and *Indian Writings in Education* (1979-1986) are important tools. NASSDOC, New Delhi, has also been working on Retrospective Indexing Project covering 240 Indian journals in social sciences; the information is available at present on documentation cards.

Newspaper Indexes

The tools covering newspapers are:

Current Indexes

1. *Bulletin on Film* (National Documentation Centre on Mass Communication, New Delhi), Quarterly.
2. *Clipping Services Bulletin* (Lalbhai Group on Rural Development, Ahmedabad), Bi-monthly.
3. *Current Press Clipping Titles* (Indian Institute of Management, Bangalore), Bi-monthly.
4. *Data India* (Press Institute of India, New Delhi), Weekly.
5. *Documentation Indian National Affairs* (Chandigarh), Quarterly.
6. *Indian Press Index* (Delhi Library Association, Delhi), Monthly.
7. *Samajik Vigyan Samachar* (NASSDOC, New Delhi), Monthly. (Since suspended).
8. *Social Science News* (NASSDOC, New Delhi), Monthly. (Since suspended).
9. *Times of India Index* (Times of India Publication, Bombay), Quarterly, (Presently suspended).

Retrospective Indexes

Kesari Shatabdi Suchi (1881-1920) (Kesari, Pune), Marathi.

Abstracting

International abstracting services in almost all disciplines of social sciences are available in hard copy and on tapes but their coverage of Indian material is meagre. To overcome this lacuna, a number of abstracting services have been taken up. These are also included in Appendix-3.

Location Services

This service consists of

(i) locating of document
(ii) locating the address of library/information centre, research institution/organisation, etc., and
(iii) locating bio-data of social scientists.

The available resource tools serving this purpose are:

DOCUMENT

It is a common experience of the researchers that great difficulty is faced in locating documents listed in the bibliographies. Union catalogues/lists lessen the ordeal to some extent. But no national Union Catalogue on books like the National Union Catalogue of the USA exists in India. NASSDOC took the initiative of compiling such catalogues/lists. Some of the catalogues/lists of this nature are:

1. *Union List of Social Science Periodicals Currently Received in...* (NASSDOC, New Delhi).

   Four volumes of the union lists covering states of Andhra Pradesh, Bombay, Delhi and Karnataka were brought out during 1971-72. The Delhi list has been continuously updated. The latest one records 2,909 periodical titles in Delhi libraries in 1985.
   The Department of Library Science of Lucknow University has compiled *Union list for Lucknow libraries*.

2. *Union Catalogue of Social Science Serials/Periodicals* (NASSDOC, New Delhi), 1970-1975, 32 vols.

   The union catalogue provides location of 31,125 serials/periodical in 535 libraries in 17 States and 2 Union Territories of India. The project undertaken on April, 1970 was completed in March 31, 1976; updating of the Union catalogue has been undertaken.

3. *Holdings of Social Science Periodicals in Libraries in Chandigarh* (ICSSR North Western Centre, Chandigarh), 1963-1984.
4. *Union Catalogue of Newspapers Available in Delhi Libraries* (NASSDOC, New Delhi).
   First brought out in 1987 and revised in 1983. Covers 252 newspaper titles in 35 libraries.

5. *Union Catalogue of Books on Library and Informatics Publications* (NASSDOC, New Delhi).
6. *Union Catalogue of Serials in Fifty-Five Academic Libraries in the State of Rajasthan.*
7. *Union List of Serials in Humanities and Social Sciences in the Libraries in Mysore City.*

ADDRESS

1. *Indian Library Directory* (Indian Library Association, New Delhi). Fourth edition (1985) covers 1595 libraries.
2. *Directory of Special and Research Libraries in India* (Indian Association of Special Libraries and Information Centres, Calcutta). Second edition covers 500 libraries.
3. *Directory of Government of India Libraries and Who's Who* (Government of India Libraries Association, *now* Association of Government Librarians and Information Specialists).
4. *Directory of Social Science Research Institutions in India* (ICSSR, New Delhi)
5. *Directory of Professional Organisations of Social Scientists in India* (ICSSR, New Delhi)
   NASSDOC updated the above two directories (4 and 5) originally published in 1971-72
6. *Directory of Social Science Research Institutions and Organisations* (ICSSR, New Delhi)
   Brought out in 1981 in cyclostyled form as part of ICSSR study on the financing of social science research in India.
7. *Inventory of Social Science Institutions and Organisations in India* (NASSDOC, New Delhi)
   Brought out in 1985. It contains addresses of over 1000 institutions/organisations.

BIO-DATA

1. *National Register of Social Scientists in India* (Concept Publishing Company, 1983, Delhi).
   ICSSR Data Archives compiled the National Register giving information of about 7000 scholars, classified under broad disciplines. The whole information of National Register is computerised and kept updated.

2. *Directory of Professors and Readers in Indian Universities, 1985* (University Grants Commission, New Delhi).

State of Art Publications

ICSSR brings out periodically survey reports on various disciplines in Social Sciences, indicating research completed, gaps identified and areas for further research. These are listed in Appendix-V.

Statistical Data Sources

Complex societal processes in modern times have made policy makers, researchers and other social scientists increasingly dependent for appropriate data. A large number of data is generated in India but it remains under-utilised.

The Sociological Research Unit of Indian Statistical Institute (Calcutta) with the financial assistance from International Social Science Council, undertook a programme (1968-1970) of surveying ongoing empirical (relying solely on observation and experiment, and not on theory) research in India for establishing an inventory of empirical data.

The ICSSR Data Archives, set up in 1973, has made efforts to inventorise quantitative data and process it into organised collection to promote and augment research. Eight data sets in machine readable form generated during the research projects funded by ICSSR and 12 data sets from those funded by other institutions have so far been collected. To provide referral services as to what kind of data is available where and in what form, the Data Archives is currently engaged in compiling an inventory of data generated since 1951 by different research institutions in India. Relevant information from 26 research institutions on 488 studies about the nature and content of data, geographical coverage, form and mode of storage, conditions and accessibility restrictions on the data, etc., have already been collected. Governmental and semi-governmental agencies are yet to be tapped and covered.

Guidance and consultancy services to social scientists involving their problems of data processing with the help of computer, are also provided by the Data Archives and some other research institutes.

Over the years, some of the research institutions have accumulated a large volume of data, and have also developed appropriate skills to handle the data processing and organisation with the help of computer technology. To involve these institutions into data organisation programme at national level, a network of institution-based data archives in India is required to be planned.

National Informatics Centre (New Delhi) which assists government departments in computerisation of their data since 1980, has succeeded in developing 150 data bases for Centre and State Government departments. It has a computer system cyber CD170/730 and a network of 20 terminals for its activities.

A large number of Governmental agencies like the National Sample Survey Organisation, Registrar General (Population Census), Reserve Bank of India and other nationalised banks, Planning Commission and State Governments have also started using computer technology for data processing.

Repository Activities

Most of the material in Social Sciences does not become obsolete from the point of view of research and as such it becomes necessary to have a repository of less used material.

In 1975-76, ICSSR in collaboration with Jawaharlal Nehru University, New Delhi, launched a project novel in this part of the world by setting up Inter-Library Resources Centre (ILRC) at New Delhi. Under the scheme the cooperating libraries deposit with ILRC their infrequently used, but important for research serials, i.e., newspapers, journals, Governmental reports, etc. This makes available at one place a large volume of research information material for scholars, and also solves the space problem. About 58 libraries at Delhi provided, as deposit and/or gift, back files of periodicals/serials to ILRC. In this way the Centre has collected about 1,00,000 volumes of periodicals/serials.

Document Supply Services

Most of the scholars live in far-off places where they do not have good information centres and library facilities. Such scholars like to have the copies of the required document at the place of their work or residence.

NASSDOC depending upon its rich resource material available in the form of periodicals, research reports and theses, etc., satisfies this demand up to 50 to 60 per cent. For the rest, NASSDOC has to depend upon other libraries in Delhi. During 1991-92, about 8,00.000 exposures from different documents were provided to the scholars including officers of ICSSR.

National Library (Calcutta) also provides documents or photocopies of the document, from its own resources as well as from foreign libraries.

Information Technology

Computers, particularly micro-computers as service media, are a common sight in information centres of the developed countries and these are extensively used for in-house activities, networking, maintaining information data bases, providing online bibliographic and textual data and operating document services. But in the developing countries, leaving aside science field, computers are not much in use.

In India some information centres, namely, Centre for Development of Instructional Technology (New Delhi), Centre for Social Development (New Delhi), ICSSR Data Archives (New Delhi), Information Centre for Development of Policy Modelling (Pune), NASSDOC (New Delhi), National Council of Applied Economic Research (New Delhi), National Informatics Centre (New Delhi), Research and Information System for Non-Aligned and Other Developing Countries (New Delhi), etc., have computer facilities for documentation and information activities. With decreasing cost of main computer and increasing availability of suitable software, this technology will gradually be more used for documentation and information activities.

Information Repackaging

Most of the information centres in India provide information and documentation services of traditional nature, and thus do not serve the information needs of the policy makers in Government and in regional and international organisations. They need information which could be readily used. Significant mobilisation activities in this direction are:

1. Research Information System for Non-Aligned and Other Developing Countries (New Delhi) brings out reviews, sum-

mary papers and analytical digests of various topics of current interest supported by data for reference by the policy-makers of the developing countries. Due attention is paid to dissemination of conclusions of and findings arrived at national and international conferences.

2. The Research and Reference Division of Parliament Library periodically brings out *Digest of Central Acts* and *Digest of Legislative and Constitutional Cases* for ready reference.

Financial Assistance

Documentation Projects

Financial assistance has been provided for a number of documentation projects. Some of these are mentioned in Appendix-6.

Library and Information Centres

Grants-in-aid has been provided to:

1. Indian Council of World Affairs, New Delhi, towards the maintenance of the library/documentation activities including subscription of journals, and
2. Indian Renaissance Institute, Dehradun, for maintenance of M.N. Roy Archives.

Publication Subsidy

Publication of good reference work has been promoted by bulk purchase of copies, for free distribution. Some of the examples in this category are:

1. *Hindi Sangrah*
2. *Index India*
3. *Index to Calcutta Review*
4. *Indian Behavioral Science Abstracts*
5. *Indian Education Index (1948-1978)*
6. *Indian Political Movement (1919-1971)*
7. *Kesari Centenary Index*
8. *Library and Information Services Index*
9. *Indian Press Index*

10. *Second Handbook of Psychological and Social Instruments.*

Study/Travel Grants

Under the scheme, the scholars are financially assisted to visit libraries in India for consulting research material, thus mobilising better use of the information sources. It will be relevant to recall in this regard what Mr. Ruth Alston, Librarian in the Cambridge University, has observed:

> "The stock of Indian libraries was significantly under-used because of user ignorance and many thought that the information profession has not, on the whole, succeeded in projecting a good image of its capabilities." (Alston, Ruth, 1983, Hunger for the Poor? Some Observations on Information Provision in India, *Journal of Information Science*, 6, p 115-22)

Data Organisation

Scholars/institutions are given financial assistance to cover expenses on items like coding, purchasing, computer time, etc., provided that the data have significant re-use potential and that the scholar/ institution is willing to give a copy of the organised data alongwith supporting documentation, namely, a copy of original questionnaire schedule, sampling design, code books, etc., to the ICSSR Data Archives to enable other interested scholars to utilise the data for secondary analysis.

Networks

Networking among science libraries and information centres has been accomplished under the National Information System in Science and Technology (NISSAT). But networking among Social Science information centres and libraries is not yet mobilised. It obtains to a certain extent in public libraries set up in States, among different libraries in university campus, and libraries of commercial undertakings like Bharat Heavy Electricals Ltd., Indian National Information System for Social Sciences (INISS) has been on the planning board for sometime. INISS, if and when established, could mobilise resources in this direction.

The network will help disseminate information about accumulated contribution to study and research of the social science scholars in the region and would ultimately enrich the pool of universal knowledge where country barriers break and one finds oneself as a partner and a co-beneficiary in a kingdom of light which belongs to the world as a whole.

Mobilisation Gaps

It will not be an exaggeration to say that Social Science information and documentation centres in India have mobilised resources and achieved a reasonable standard in information services. There are, nonetheless, gaps too, and the priority areas, already requiring immediate attention are:

1. There is still no exhaustive bibliographical control of

   (i) non-doctoral research, both completed and in progress,
   (ii) working papers, and
   (iii) reports submitted at the conferences/seminars/workshops;

2. There is insufficient analytical type of documentation and informations activity;
3. Indian National Information System for Social Sciences network towards cooperative partaking of information resources at tremendous savings in costs is not shaping;
4. Data archival activities for mobilization of resources are still at the nascent stage; and
5. There appears no visible impact of modern information technology on information services management. Inhibiting factors include lack of:

   (i) suitable software,
   (ii) trained manpower in system management, and above all
   (iii) financial resources.

6. The role of Social Science Information as an important input resource for the socio-economic development is not yet fully recognised.

International Enhancement

Input Centres

There are some organisations which act as input centres for international data bases. Some of these are:

I. NASSDOC provides input data regarding Indian publications to—

(i) International Committee for Social Science Information and Documentation (ICSSID), Paris for *International Bibliographies* in the field of Anthropology, Economics, Political Science and Sociology;
(ii) *International Bulletin for Bibliography of Education*, Madrid,
(iii) *International Geographical Bibliography*, Paris,

II. NASSDOC also updated inventories of Indian Social Science research institutions, journals and research projects completed and in progress for DARE DATA BANK of UNESCO, and

III. NASSDOC was also approached to extend geographical coverage to Asia-Pacific region, as NASSDOC was actively involved in Asia-Pacific Information Network in Social Sciences (APINESS), and project assigned and taken up in the context include:

1. *India 2000: An Annotated Bibliography*;
2. *Selective Inventory of Information Services*;
3. Collecting data from Asia-Pacific region for *World Directory of Social Science Institutions*; and
4. State of the Art report on Social Science research trends in India.

The Centre for Development of Instructional Technology (New Delhi) and the Indian Council of Agricultural Research (New Delhi) are input centres for DEVSIS and AGRIS systems respectively.

The ICSSR Data Archives is a member of International Federation of Data Organisations (IFDO) and is the regional secretariat of the International Association for Social Science Information Services and Technology (IASSIST). A plan for exchange of data and software with several IFDO member archives is being worked out. Possibilities are also being explored for undertaking with other IFDO member archives, joint projects of mutual interest.

Exchange of Resources

NASSDOC has agreements with well over 2000 Indian and foreign Institutions for exchange of publications as well grey and unconventional material. List of exchange partners in Asia and the Pacific is given in Appendix-VII.

Action Outline

Information system in the development field have been mobilized and are available at national level with interlinkages where possible. However, there is a need for dissemination of information about available resources, data bases/networks. And, we have also to oversee:

(i) better coordination of information resources via institutions and centres;
(ii) effective communication of information resources to practising librarians, information scientists and information brokers;
(iii) mechanism to identify suitable information personnel with missionary zeal, and their training to work efficiently as system analysts, database managers, computer hardware/software specialists, etc.;
(iv) back-up and judicious use of financial resources;
(v) easy availability of information exactly what a specialist needs, no more and no less; and
(vi) better mechanism to identify, record and notify information resources.

PART III

EXPOSITION

3

INDIAN PERIODICALS IN SOCIAL SCIENCES

Introduction

As foundation of scholarship, periodical literature occupies an important place in social sciences. Journals seek to disseminate knowledge and enable researchers to publish their work, to become familiar with the work of others and to benefit from scholarly discussions and dialogues. In fact without journals, it is difficult to ensure the growth of any research discipline. As a discipline grows, the volume of research grows and the need for more journals to publish the research findings, becomes increasingly felt. Thus the number of research journals in a discipline is one indicator of its status and growth. In India, publication of social science journals increased correspondingly with the growth in research institutions/organisations. Before 1947 when the research activity was confined only to university departments and a few research institutions/associations, the number of learned journals in social sciences was also small. Analysis of the growth rate of social science journals decade-wise, the number of journals discipline-wise, counting multi-disciplinary journals in all disciplines, and geographical area covered respectively, based on data collected for UNESCO DARE system during 1982 is shown in Tables 3.1, 3.2 and 3.3 respectively.

Contents

Most of the contributors to social science press are academics and their editors are professionals who have a good background and training in social sciences. A study made in 1964 of 10 journals shows that almost 80 per cent of the articles were found to be informative, about 15 per cent analytical with theoretical significance, while only 5 per cent had articles on policy formulation. According to the same study, the contributors to the social sciences were largely academics, very few bureaucrats and still fewer active social and political workers. Of a total of 315 contributors, 294 were academicians, 19 bureaucrats and only two social and political workers. These journals were mostly owned by learned societies, universities, educational institutions, etc.

TABLE 3.1: Period of Starting of New Journals

	Period	No. of Journals
1.	Up to 1900	3
2.	1901 to 1910	1
3.	1911 to 1920	3
4.	1921 to 1930	5
5.	1931 to 1940	6
6.	1941 to 1950	6
7.	1951 to 1960	46
8.	1961 to 1970	71
9.	1971 to 1980	102
10.	1981	12
11.	1982	9
12.	1983	1
	Total	265

TABLE 3.2: Subject-wise Distribution of Journals

	Discipline	No. of Journals
1.	Accounting	1
2.	Administration	1
3.	Adult Education	2
4.	Africa	5
5.	Agricultural Economics	1
6.	Agriculture	2
7.	America (U.S.)	2
8.	Andhra Pradesh	1
9.	Anthropology	6
10.	Applied Psychology	1
11.	Archaeology	1
12.	Asia	7
13.	Australia	1

Contd.

	Discipline	No. of Journals
14.	Behavioural Sciences	2
15.	China (People's Republic)	1
16.	Clinical Psychology	1
17.	Comparative Law	2
18.	Constitutional Law	2
19.	Consumer	2
20.	Cooperatives	6
21.	Criminology	2
22.	Culture	2
23.	Democracy	2
24.	Demography	2
25.	Development	4
26.	Economic Development	11
27.	Economics	19
28.	Education	20
29.	Educational Psychology	2
30.	Energy	1
31.	Europe	1
32.	Family	2
33.	Folklore	1
34.	Futurology	2
35.	Gandhiana	1
36.	Geography	6
37.	Health	1
38.	Higher Education	3
39.	History	4
40.	Humanities	2
41.	India	6
42.	Indian Ocean	1
43.	Indology	1
44.	Industrial Relations	1
45.	Industry	3
46.	Information System	5
47.	International Affairs	8
48.	International Law	1
49.	Islam	2
50.	Japan	1
51	Korea	1
52.	Labour	3
53.	Law	7
54.	Linguistics	4
55.	Local Government	4
56.	Maharashtra	2
57.	Management	7

Contd

	Discipline	No. of Journals
58.	Manpower	2
59.	Mass Communication	2
60.	Mental Retardation	1
61.	Mongolia	1
62.	Orissa	1
63.	Parliamentary System	4
64.	Philosophy	4
65.	Political Science	8
66.	Politics	1
67.	Productivity	2
68.	Psychology	11
69.	Public Administration	8
70.	Public Enterprises	1
71.	Public Opinion	1
72.	Punjab	1
73.	Rural Development	10
74.	Rural Industry	1
75.	Rural Planning	1
76.	Science	2
77.	Science Policy	1
78.	Social Anthropology	1
79.	Social Change	1
80.	Social Science	18
81.	Social Services	2
82.	Social Welfare	2
83.	Social Work	1
84.	Society	1
85.	Sociology	14
86.	Statistics	2
87.	Teaching	4
88.	Technology	1
89.	Tourism	2
90.	Urban Planning	1
91.	Women	1
	Total	305

Users

Academic libraries are the largest clientele of the learned journals. Serious reading in India is limited to research scholars, professionals, academicians, policy-makers and administrators. An average reader seldom uses these journals for information and enlightenment. He finds himself comfortable in the company of general type of periodicals, presenting information in a simple way.

Thus, it will be seen that there are only a small number of users and even these do not fully utilise the documentary materials appearing in these journals. This is mainly due to lack of bibliographical control over the periodical material. International abstracting and indexing journals do include Indian journals but their coverage is very small. However, of late, documentation activity in this direction is expanding. Indian Council of Social Science Research took up a project of indexing of about 240 Indian social science periodicals since the first volume of each periodical to the year 1970.

Index to Indian Periodicals: Sociology and Psychology, 1886-1970, covering 35 journals in Sociology (1886-1970) and 7 journals in Psychology (1926-1970) was published in 1987. Prior to this, Indian Institute of Education, Pune, with the cooperation of Indian Council of Social Science Research published in 1980, *Indian Education Index, 1947-1978*, covering 26 journals in Education. Quite recently in 1991, CICIL series included *Indian Writings on Education* covering 31 journals (1979 to 1986).

TABLE 3.3: Geographical Area Covered

	Geographical Area	No. of Journals
1.	International	117
2.	Africa	7
3.	Asia	14
4.	Australia	1
5.	China	1
6.	Developing Nations	1
7.	Europe	1
8.	India	131
9.	North America	1
	Total	274

The academic standard of Indian journals compares well with the foreign journals, particularly in the field of Economics and Industrial Relations. But, inexplicably, while costly foreign journals are being subscribed to by most of the academic libraries, subscription to Indian journals is very poor. Even some highly specialised Indian journals are not received by some university libraries.

The sorry state of affairs can be due only to lack of up-to-date directories of Indian periodicals and injudicious subscription policy as a result of non-coordination in resource sharing and formulation of subscription policy. Compilation of Union lists/catalogues greatly helps in improving this unhealthy situation. ICSSR brought out Union catalogue of Social Science periodicals/serials in libraries in India (32 volumes) and periodically compiled union lists of periodicals currently received in libraries.

Publication Health of Journals

Due to lack of periodicals directories, it is difficult to know the exact number of existing publications. The high death rate of periodicals is also astonishing and negates efforts to arrive at an accurate figure. Besides the birth rate of new periodicals is on the low side, thanks to the prohibitive cost of paper and printing. As if this was not enough, marketing hurdles block circulation prospects and advertisers, who are nourishing resources, keep miles away. Academic journals are frequently shy of courting advertisements thinking rightly or wrongly that academics should keep themselves scrupulously out of non-academic or commercial pursuits. Price escalation to the extent of 100 per cent keeps away the medium-size libraries from subscribing to the journals, although, "periodicals published in India are reasonably priced and their price graph does not tend to rise too steeply for variety of reasons. Considerable proportion of Indian periodical publications are brought out by governmental agencies, besides academic and research institutions. Periodicals brought out by agencies with commercial motivation are equally cautious in this respect. Considerable proportion of their subscription list is confined to Indian clientele who cannot afford too violent variations in prices. It is also a captive audience. Unfortunately, there is no ready-made data available of the price graph of Indian social science periodicals during the previous decade for comparative purpose." (Girja Kumar and Jayaswal, 1982). The publication is increasingly becoming a highly skilled professional job with almost unlimited resources to draw upon. If these assets are lacking, a periodical will find the going rough, if not impossible, with the result that its survival will soon be at stake. Government and private institutional financial assistance is a must for the survival of the academic journals and keeping higher professional standards.

Statistical Analysis*

There are at present 15,995 periodicals in circulation in the country and information regarding their nature of contents was available in respect of 14,248 periodicals. These journals have been classified into 21 subject categories based on their contents.

The largest number of periodicals (5,862) came under the category of News and Current Affairs followed by Commerce and Industry (1,596), Social Welfare (426) and so on. Periodicity-wise, weeklies among the News and Current Affairs periodicals were the largest in number while monthlies were the largest in other social science periodicals (Table 3.4).

TABLE 3.4: Periodicity-wise Number of Periodicals according to Contents, 1979

Category	Weeklies	Fortnightlies	Monthlies	Quarterlies	Other periodicities	Annuals	Total
News and Current Affairs	3919	1147	660	72	45	19	5862
Commerce and Industry	70	56	314	95	41	20	596
Social Welfare	43	51	229	80	23	—	426
Labour	33	55	220	22	9	—	339
Education	9	33	127	77	43	8	297
Law and Public Administration	24	50	174	39	11	4	302
Children	9	20	138	13	8	4	192
Transport and Communication	4	6	71	11	3	4	99
Insurance, Banking and Co-operation	18	11	54	25	7	1	119
Finance and Economics	10	12	42	19	17	3	103
Women	9	8	52	7	6	3	85

In the social science fields, journals were mostly being published in English, Hindi, Assamese, Bengali, Gujarati, Kannada, Malayalam, Marathi and Punjabi (Table 3.5).

* Based on *Press in India* 1980, Pt. II.

TABLE 3.5: Language-wise Number of Periodicals according to Contents, 1979

Category	English	Hindi	Assamese	Bengali	Gujarati	Kannada	Kashmiri	Malayalam	Marathi	Oriya	Punjabi
News and Current Affairs	590	2732	19	408	101	89	—	74	184	30	148
Commerce and Industry	420	41	—	5	6	3	—	3	6	—	—
Social Welfare	89	118	1	16	64	5	—	1	29	3	3
Labour	100	69	—	10	9	2	—	3	10	3	4
Education	103	37	2	13	18	10	—	3	15	1	—
Law and Public Administration	227	16	—	3	3	1	—	1	10	1	1
Children	12	44	1	32	11	3	—	12	10	5	3
Transport Communication	59	10	—	4	1	1	—	1	2	2	1
Insurance, Banking and Co-operation	47	15	—	1	3	4	—	—	14	1	1
Finance and Economics	81	10	—	—	1	1	—	—	1	—	—
Women	22	21	—	3	13	—	—	5	6	—	1
	1750	3113	23	495	230	119	—	103	287	46	162
									Total		6328

News and Current Affairs journals with a combined circulation of 9,423,000 were at the top followed by Finance and Economics (775,000), Commerce and Industry (585,000) and so on (Table 3.6).

Language-wise break-up of circulation in each category is given in Table 3.7.

Tables 3.8 and 3.9 show periodicity-wise and language-wise respectively the number of periodicals for which data were available.

Information was available about the contents of 532 of the 558 periodicals published by the Central and State Governments. More than 100 (112) came under the category of News and Current Affairs. Sixty-eight journals were dealing with Social Welfare. Those under Agriculture and Animal Husbandry numbered 52. There were 42 journals in the field of Commerce and Industry.

Government publications were brought out in all but two of the

21 categories. There was no Film journal or Sports magazine. All the periodicals in the category of Radio and Music, Art and Women were owned by the Central Government. On the other hand, the only periodical belonging to Religion and Philosophy was published by a State Government (Table 3.10).

TABLE 3.6: Periodicity-wise Circulation of Periodicals according to Contents, 1979
(in Thousands)

Category	Weeklies	Fortnightlies	Monthlies	Quarterlies	Other periodicities	Annuals	Total
News and Current Affairs	7012	1390	878	73	19	51	9423
Commerce and Industry	114	49	280	58	29	55	585
Social Welfare	41	46	347	28	13	—	475
Labour	19	55	258	76	3	—	411
Education	17	19	158	81	49	6	330
Law and Public Administration	43	53	261	40	2	—	399
Children	121	563	1708	3	2	13	2410
Transport and Communication	8	3	186	18	—	—	215
Insurance, Banking and Co-operation	28	8	123	147	10	—	316
Finance and Economics	51	21	74	8	6	—	160

TABLE 3.7: Language-wise Circulation of Periodicals according to Contents, 1979

Category	English	Hindi	Assamese	Bengali	Gujarati	Kannada	Malayalam	Marathi	Oriya	Punjabi	Sanskrit
News and Current Affairs	1887	3537	64	587	266	242	215	277	18	306	—
Commerce and Industry	441	53	—	16	6	1	1	7	—	—	—
Social Welfare	125	184	—	10	56	10	10	15	2	7	—
Labour	131	59	—	17	6	—	—	6	6	—	—
Education	64	88	—	11	20	10	4	10	—	—	—

(Contd.)

TABLE 3.7 *(Contd.)*

Category	English	Hindi	Assamese	Bengali	Gujarati	Kannada	Malayalam	Marathi	Oriya	Punjabi	Sanskrit
Law and Public Administration	303	13	—	—	4	2	1	25	1	—	—
Children	192	870	4	296	122	102	298	123	42	5	—
Transport and Communication	103	21	—	7	—	—	—	64	—	—	—
Finance and Economics	132	6	—	—	13	—	—	—	—	—	—
Women	318	22	—	2	141	—	194	22	—	—	—
Insurance, Banking and Co-operation	222	12	—	1	8	2	—	24	—	5	—

TABLE 3.7 *(Contd.)*

Category	Sindhi	Tamil	Telugu	Urdu	Bi-Lingual	Multi Lingual	Other	Total
News and Current Affairs	44	507	249	808	333	43	35	9123
Commerce and Industry	—	1	—	1	49	9	—	585
Social Welfare	—	10	10	6	22	7	1	435
Labour	—	26	1	1	103	1	—	354
Education	—	4	12	4	91	11	1	330
Law and Public Administration	—	14	20	1	15	—	—	399
Children	—	134	173	16	20	8	5	2430
Transport and Communication	—	2	13	—	2	3	—	215
Finance and Economics	—	3	—	—	6	—	—	160
Women	—	36	13	26	1	—	—	775
Insurance, Banking and Co-operation	—	12	4	2	8	16	—	316

TABLE 3.8: Periodicity-wise Number of Periodicals according to Contents for which Circulation was Available, 1979

Category	Weeklies	Fortnightlies	Monthlies	Quarterlies	Other periodicities	Annuals	Total
News and Current Affairs	1715	452	267	36	15	11	2496
Commerce and Industry	35	26	154	38	24	6	283
Social Welfare	21	24	107	37	13	—	202
Labour	13	25	94	8	2	—	142
Education	4	9	68	42	14	4	141
Law and Public Administration	12	33	97	24	4	—	170
Children	6	11	79	3	2	3	104
Transport and Communication	3	4	37	6	1	—	51
Insurance, Banking and Co-operation	13	5	37	15	4	—	74
Finance and Economics	7	4	21	10	8	—	50
Women	5	5	22	3	1	1	37

TABLE 3.9: Language-wise Number of Periodicals according to Contents for which Circulation was Available, 1979

Category	English	Hindi	Assamese	Bengali	Gujarati	Kannada	Kashmiri	Malayalam	Marathi	Oriya	Punjabi
News & Current Affairs	248	1057	11	234	59	43	—	34	89	14	69
Commerce & Industry	207	18	—	3	4	2	—	2	3	—	—
Social Welfare	52	44	—	9	35	2	—	1	12	1	1
Labour	49	22	—	8	5	—	—	1	5	1	—
Education	50	17	—	7	10	4	—	1	7	—	—
Law & Public Administration	128	11	—	—	4	1	—	1	5	1	—
Children	8	17	1	18	6	3	—	7	7	2	2
Transport & Communication	32	7	—	2	—	—		2	—	—	—
Insurance, Banking and Co-operation	26	10	—	1	2	2	—		10	—	1
Finance and Economics	40	3	—	—	1	—	—	—	1	—	—
Women	7	6	—	2	8	—	—	2	3	—	—

TABLE 3.9 *(Contd.)*

Category	Sanskrit	Sindhi	Tamil	Telugu	Urdu	Bi-Lingual	Multi Lingual	Others	Total
News and Current Affairs	1	10	40	57	305	182	25	18	2496
Commerce and Industry	—	—	1	—	1	34	8	—	283
Social Welfare	—	—	6	4	5	21	8	1	202
Labour	—	—	—	2	2	38	2	—	142
Education	—	—	4	4	4	25	7	1	141
Law and Public Administration	—	—	3	4	1	10	1	—	170
Children	—	—	9	7	7	4	3	3	104
Transport and Communication	—	—	1	2	—	3	2	—	51
Insurance, Banking and Co-operation	—	—	9	1	—	8	4	—	74
Finance and Economics	—	—	1	—	—	4	—	—	50
Women	—	—	2	1	5	1	—	—	37

TABLE 3.10: Content-wise Number of Government Publications, 1979

Category	Central Government	State Government	Total
News and Current Affairs	48	64	112
Social Welfare	21	47	68
Commerce and Industry	32	10	42
Education	11	26	37
Transport and Communication	32	2	34
Law and Public Administration	10	11	21
Finance and Economics	2	7	9
Insurance, Banking and Co-operation	—	2	2
Women	2	—	2
Children	1	1	2
Religion and Philosophy	—	1	1

BACKGROUNDERS

Chiva, I., 1974, Scholarly Periodicals: Their Strength and Weaknesses, *International Social Science Journal* 26(3), p. 372-392.

Dhawli, Anand S. and Ghosh, Amitabh, 1979, A Study of the Image of Indian Journals on Management and Social Sciences in the International Academic Community, *Journal of Higher Education*, 4(3), Spring, p. 313-326.

Girija Kumar and Jayaswal, P.K., 1982, Social Science Periodicals in Libraries, *Library Herald 21*(1-2) April-September, p. 1-27.

Rawat, Taj, 1982, Publishing Higher Educational Journals, *Indian Book Industry* 27(11), p. 15-16.

Narender Kumar, 1984, Citation Study as a Tool for Evaluation of Journal Collection on Use: A Case Study, *Journal of Library Information* 9(1) June, p. 48-64.

Subbarao, C.V., et al, 1985, Periodical Resources and Balancing Budgets, *ILA Bulletin* 20(3-4) October-March, p. 135-155.

Subrahmanya, K.N., 1985, Economic publications: Old and New: Why some succeed as other fold up? *Southern Economist*, 24, November 15, p. 37-40.

4

INDIAN DISSERTATIONS IN SOCIAL SCIENCES

Scope

Social Science subjects here include Commerce, Economics, Education, Geography, History, Law, Management, Political Science, Psychology, Public Administration and Sociology. The bibliographical tools encompassing all disciplines including social sciences and broader areas including India have been covered. The dissertations on India submitted to foreign universities have also been taken care of. The terms "Dissertation" and "Thesis" have been used interchangeably. However, dissertations submitted in partial fulfilment of the requirements for a higher degree in conjunction with a written examination have been excluded.

Introduction

It is generally agreed that the developed world has made tremendous progress in Science and Technology which has enabled it to adopt ways and means for achieving higher standards of living, while the under-developed world is struggling for the same. How has the developed world succeeded in better means of prosperity? – It is through higher standards in research. Research is done in universities, laboratories, research institutes, etc. The research findings appear in the form of dissertations, research reports and research articles.

Definition

There is generally not much divergence of opinion about the definition of the term "Dissertation/Thesis" as is evident from the two definitions given below:

> "A substantial paper that is submitted to the faculty of a university by a candidate for an advanced degree that is typically based on independent research and that if acceptable usually gives evidence of the candidate's mastery both of his own subject and scholarly method". (*Webster's Third New International Dictionary*).

> "A statement of investigation of research presenting the author's finding and conclusions reached and submitted by the author in support of his candidature for a higher degree, professional qualification or other award". (Peter, 1980).

Dissertations and theses submitted to various universities and institutions of advanced learning constitute invaluable information sources to research workers. They find in these dissertations the data and results already arrived at and relevant to their research work. These reports show the scholar's grasp of a given subject and the research methodology involved. Sometimes theses are published in amended form or appear in the form of articles which are consulted and cited by the scholars, in the literature.

Bibliographical Control

A large number of doctoral degrees are awarded annually by universities and research institutions deemed as universities all over the world. An idea about their number can be had from the bibliographical tools listing them. *Comprehensive Dissertation Index 1861-1972* by University Microfilms gives information of over 417,000 dissertations approved by universities in the USA and Canada in all the disciplines. *Index to Theses 1982* by ASLIB, lists above 8,402 items. (Patterson and Hardy, 1982). In India, the Association of Indian Universities (*formerly* Inter-University Board of India and Ceylon) took initiative towards bibliographical control of dissertations produced in India as early as in 1935 by bringing out a list covering the period from 1930-1934. There was no differentiation of subjects in the list published at intervals of two/three years for a period of approximately a quarter century. The consolidated lists covering the period, 1857-1970, and 1971-1975 were brought out in 1974 and 1979 respectively. These lists have been kept up-to-date by annual supplements. A decade-wise and subject-wise growth of doctorates awarded by Indian universities up to 1980 is given in Table 4.1. It not only shows the number of doctorates awarded but also the growth of research work on various disciplines in social sciences. The total number of dissertations listed comes to about 8,795.

TABLE 4.1: Subject-wise and Year-wise Distribution of Dissertations in Social Sciences accepted by Indian Universities 1857-1980

Subject	Upto 1920	1921 to 1930	1931 to 1940	1941 to 1950	1951 to 1960	1961 to 1970	1971 to 1980	Total
Commerce	—	—	2	7	35	78	84	306
Economics	3	4	17	71	293	647	1253	2289
Education	—	—	—	10	79	233	854	1176
Geography	—	—	—	—	—	—	360	360
History*	—	—	—	—	—	—	1012	1012
Law	7	3	1	3	11	42	141	208
Management	—	—	—	2	15	65	226	308
Political Science	–	3	5	13	83	285	598	990
Psychology	—	1	2	3	36	169	451	662
Public Administration	—	—	1	12	34	103	252	402
Sociology	—	1	5	39	98	292	656	1082
Total	10	12	33	160	684	1904	5987	8795

* Information available for the period 1971-80

Note: Year of Award of Degree is not available for the following number of subjects of Lucknow University:
Economics—1; Political Science—3; Sociology—1

Source: Bibliography of Doctoral Dissertations: Social Sciences and Humanities, 1957/1970-1979/1980. Association of Indian Universities, New Delhi. (Includes cumulative and annual supplements).

Efforts at individual and institutional levels are thus made in all the countries to have bibliographic control of this important grey material. In India, university libraries are prominent in compiling the lists of theses retained by them. In addition to these university libraries, Association of Indian Universities, as explained before, has been doing useful work in the field. ASLIB in the U.K. and University Microfilms in the U.S.A. are working towards this end. The reference tools containing material of this nature generally appear in the form of (i) classified lists of titles with or without annotations, aided by suitable indexes, and/or (ii) abstracts of theses arranged under broad subject readings with suitable indexes. These lists may further appear periodically or published ad-hoc covering retrospectively at fixed period. The subject coverage may range from one subject to a group of subjects and even comprising all disciplines of knowledge. The bibliographical information provided by each entry normally includes: the scholar's name; the title; the name of institution awarding the degree; year of degree awarded and in its absence year of submission of the thesis; the name of the guide and abstract (only in case of abstracting publications). Some of these reference lists are given in the Appendix-IV, supplemented by Appendix IV-A.

Availability

Unlike other published monographic materials, it is not easy to obtain dissertations/theses through the usual commercial publishing channel. Further, a limited number of copies usually in typed form are submitted to the universities. The holding institutions are, therefore, reluctant to provide these on inter-library loan. Theses can be consulted only in the library premises and this thus restricts their use. It becomes even more difficult for the researchers to make use of theses if available at different centres. Special efforts are, therefore, required to be made to know about their existence and procurement, if so desired.

Global View

In 1954, the Standing Conference of National and University Libraries (SCONUL), Great Britain, proposed a fourfold standard of availability for theses (Patterson and Hardy, 1982):

(a) At least one copy of every thesis should be deposited in the University Library,
(b) Subject to the author's consent every thesis should be available for inter-library loan,
(c) Subject to author's consent, every thesis should be available for photo-copying, and
(d) Authors of theses should be asked at the time of deposit to give their consent in writing to (b) and (c) and this consent should be inserted in the deposited copy of theses.

As a consequence of these efforts, British Library Lending Division (BLLD) has, since 1970, been trying to increase the utilisation of British doctoral theses by microfilming the theses of those universities which have agreed to participate in an experiment to build up a central collection. The availability of theses is known from *BLLD Announcement Bulletin*. Photocopies and microfilm copies are available for loan or retention. About 40,000 British doctoral theses in all disciplines are available at present under the scheme.

In the United States, more than 370 cooperating institutions provide abstracts of dissertations retained by them to University Microfilms Inc. The abstracts are reported, as already mentioned, in *Dissertation Abstracts International*. The dissertations are available for purchase either in Microfilm or in Xerographic text from the publisher.

National Scene

The National Social Science Documentation Centre (NASSDOC) in India has devised a scheme to create a document base of dissertations. Under the scheme, the doctoral scholars are invited to deposit a copy of their theses along with its abstract at NASSDOC against a token payment of Rs. 400. NASSDOC has so far collected about 2,500 theses, and this will gradually go on increasing. To make room for incoming research material, NASSDOC started getting the theses microfilmed.

The scholars visiting NASSDOC can consult the theses of various universities at one place and with availability of photocopying facilities at the NASSDOC, can get photocopies of the relevant material. Indian Council of Social Science Research has six regional centres: Bombay, Calcutta, Chandigarh, Delhi, Hyderabad, and Shillong. (Appendix-VIII). Each Centre has been authorised to purchase a copy of the theses in its respective regional language(s).

In the days to come NASSDOC is expected to collect a large number of theses, striving to provide not only consultation facilities, but also to provide microfilm or photo-copy of the document for loan and purchase. This will be possible only with the cooperation of concerned universities and scholars by taking steps on the lines suggested by SCONUL (Great Britain).

BACKGROUNDERS

Eswara Reddy, D.B., n.d., *South Asian Agricultural Dissertations Documentation Centre : A Microfilming Project : Paper Presented at 11th IASLIC National Seminar*, Hyderabad, 4 p. Mimeographed.

Gidwani, N.N. and Navalani, K., comps and eds., 1974, *A Guide to Reference Materials on India*, Saraswati Pub., Jaipur, p. 65-69.

Ming, Ding Choo, 1984, Access to Dissertations in and on South-East Asia, *Libri* 34(2), p. 88-112.

Patterson, Geoffrey M. and Hardy, Joan E., eds., 1982, *Index to Theses Accepted for Higher Degrees*, London, ASLIB, vol. 31, pt. 1.

Peter, Auger C., 1980, Reports and Theses, Conferences and Symposia, Standards and Patents, *In* : Higgens, Gavin, ed., 1980, *Printed Reference Material*, Oxford and IBH, New Delhi, p. 233.

Ramaiah, L.S. and Prafulla Chandra, T.V., 1985, Research Dissertations: Problems of Acquisition, *Herald of Library Science* 24(3), p. 202-206.

Webster's Third New International Dictionary, G and C Merriam Co., Springfield, Mass., p. 656.

5

INDIAN GOVERNMENT DOCUMENTS

Government publication had been generally defined as a document published at the expense of the government and/or published under the authority of law.

In the present age of democratic set-up, the activities of the governments have increased manifold. This has resulted in generation of voluminous literature which interests the layman as well as the expert depending upon the thought content and the style of presentation.

In India – the biggest democratic country – a large number of official publications are brought out annually. The Department of Publication of Government of India singly handles 75,000 titles of 184 Departments, Ministries, Attached and Subordinate offices of the Central Government including semi-government and autonomous institutions and organisations. Another important department which deals with the publication and sale of official documents is the Publication Division of the Ministry of Information and Broadcasting which has so far brought out about 5,800 publications. Parliament secretariat also markets a large number of publications.

Leaving aside publications brought out for publicity or for education of the layman, much of the material is rich in descriptive information and statistical data about the natural resources and development programmes of our country. They cover several of the key and significant areas of our national life. Their importance as primary sources of research is beyond doubt. Further, the source is less costly in comparison to similar type of publications brought out by non-official channels.

In spite of their usefulness, these are not available to a large number of researchers. The paradoxical situation applies both to the publications of the Central Government and State Governments – acutely to the State Governments.

Endeavour here is to present the prevailing situation and to identify bottlenecks and to suggest measures to remove them in the context of marketing and utilisation of Government of India publications. It is felt that the remedial measures applied in the case of Government of India publications can be fairly applied in the case of State Government publications as well.

Nature of Publications

Different types of official publications are brought out which can be broadly grouped as under:

1. Administration Reports;
2. Research Reports (Census Reports, Survey Reports, Statistical Digests, Committees and Commissions Reports);
3. Law Reports (Judicial Decisions, Acts, Laws, Rules and Regulations);
4. Parliamentary Proceedings (including Reports of Parliamentary Committees);
5. Periodicals;
6. Maps;
7. Leaflets, Brochures, Booklets, Commemoration and Centenary volumes, Tourist Guides, etc.

Generation Sources

1. Ministries/Departments of the Government and their sub-offices;
2. Parliamentary bodies;
3. Statutory organisations like Election Commission of India, Office of the Comptroller General of India, Union Public Service Commission, Office of the Attorney General of India, Office of the Commissioner for Scheduled Castes and Scheduled Tribes, etc.;
4. Judicial Bodies like Supreme Court and High Courts;
5. Committees and Commissions appointed by the Government.

Present Position

BIBLIOGRAPHICAL TOOLS

The following bibliographical tools, among others, provide current information about government publications :

Accession List: South Asia
(U.S. Library of Congress Office, New Delhi). Monthly.
Catalogue : Government of India Civil Publications
(Controller of Publications, Delhi). Monthly.
Catalogue of Government of India Civil Publications, corrected up to . . .
(Controller of Publications, Delhi). Irregular.
Latest covers the period upto 1st January, 1991.
Indian Books
(Mukherji Book House, Calcutta). Monthly.
Lists selected official titles in each issue.
Indian National Bibliography
(Central Reference Library, Calcutta). Monthly.
Parliament Library Bulletin
(Parliament Library, Reference, Research, Documentation and Information Service, New Delhi). Weekly.

Resource Centres

Some of the government libraries in Delhi — Central Secretariat Library, Ministry of Home Affairs, Ministry of Finance, Parliament, and Planning Commission, etc., are depository libraries for Government of India publications. Besides these libraries, National Library (Calcutta), Connemara Public Library (Madras), Central Library (Bombay) and Delhi Public Library (Delhi) receive one copy each of the government publications under the Delivery of Books Act, 1954. A few research libraries in the country — Indian Institute of Public Administration Library (Delhi), National Archives Library (Delhi), Archaeological Survey of India Library (Delhi), National Council of Agricultural Research Library (Delhi), National Council of Applied Economic Research Library (Delhi) and Gokhale Institute of Politics and Economics (Pune) also keep a good number of government publications.

Research Facilities

The researchers can consult the available material in the departmental libraries. *The Directory of Government of India Libraries*, compiled by the erstwhile Government of India Librarians Association, (*now* Association of Government Librarians and Information) in 1984 can be helpful identifying the libraries retaining the desired specialised material and also the services offered by them. But it is not always easy to have access to these centres due to entry restrictions. Further, the primary objective of these centres is to serve their internal clientele, and as such outside scholars do not receive much cooperation and encouragement. It is the general experience of scholars that locating the old official documents in these libraries is very difficult and in case located, it is further difficult to have these on loan for study and noting. Satisfactory reprographic facilities are also not available. It may appear strange, but it is a fact that Indian scholars visit foreign libraries to consult the old records.

Marketing of Publications

The position is face to face with publication programme handling as mentioned in the beginning. The Controller of Publications is the most important organ of the government responsible for publication and marketing of the largest number of the official documents. It is estimated that 75 per cent of the Government of India publications are handled by it through its 896 sales agents (including 24 foreign agents, 150 Sale and Return Agents and 365 Employment Exchanges). The other two important publication agencies are, Publication Division of the Ministry of Information and Broadcasting, and Parliament Secretariat (Lok Sabha and Rajya Sabha). Both the agencies have a network of sales depots, sales counters, agencies and distribution offices.

In the capital city Delhi, it is rather easier to get these publications on cash payment. But for institutions situated in far-off places, it is very difficult first to keep track of the new releases by various departments and when known, to acquire these from the concerned sponsors. The supply procedures are so slow that it takes a couple of months (and sometimes more) to get an indented title. And it takes many more months to get refund of the payment against non-supply of the material. The experience of the institutions in dealings with the Controller of Publications is not a happy one. Some of the books reported to be out of stock are later weeded out and find their way to the commercial market, and can be had at a premium. This can happen only with the connivance of some unscrupulous employees in the office. To intimate the users about the new releases, the Controller of Publications issues periodically *Catalogue of Government of India Civil Publications*. But the number of printed copies is reported to be sometimes about 500 or 1000 which is too small in comparison to the number of user institutions. Some of the new releases are also advertised in the national newspapers. *Accession List: South Asia* and *Indian National Bibliography* as listed earlier are the other two tools which list new arrivals. Most Ministers/Departments also bring out their own catalogues of publications.

REMEDIAL MEASURES

It is, by and large, opined that in spite of large expenditure incurred on the compilation and publication of the documents, these are not put to maximum use. Slow marketing techniques, lack of information and consultation facilities are greatly responsible for this. Following measures may help alleviate the situation.

Bibliographical Control

Parliament Library at Delhi should be made responsible for full bibliographical control of publications. There are sound reasons for this. It has sufficient financial and manpower resources. It receives copies of all the official documents published/unpublished and priced/non-priced, emanating from any source, as these are required to be placed in Parliament. Therefore, it is not faced with acquisition problems which others like the Controller of Publications which compiles *Catalogue of Government of India Civil Publications* and Central Reference Library, Calcutta, compiler of *Indian National Bibliography (INB)*, face particularly in the case of unpublished documents.

It would not be unfair, if *INB* coverage is restricted to non-official documents and the bibliographical control of this material is taken up by Parliament Library.

Financial assistance should be provided to individuals/institutions who intend to take up documentation projects in this field. Indian Council of Social Science Research (ICSSR), New Delhi, realising the importance of the work, provided financial assistance to the Indian Institute of Public Administration (IIPA), New Delhi, for "Study of the publications, bibliographic and distribution mechanism of the State Governments and compilation of a select bibliography of State

Governments publications". The Project Director, Shri Mohinder Singh, who has to his credit the publication of *Government of India Publications*, has brought out *State Government Publications in India, 1947-1982*, in two volumes, which is based on the above study.

Resource Centres

More resource centres in the form of Reference Centres/Depository Centres/and Clearing House Centres are required for maximum utilisation of literature. Suggested Centres are:

National Reference Library for Government Documents

It should have the following activities:

(i) to acquire one copy each of all the official documents (published/mimeographed);
(ii) to provide facilities to bona-fide research scholars for consultation;
(iii) to provide photo-copying facilities to the users. In case of out-of-prints, photocopy of the complete document may be provided;
(iv) to get the old records converted into micro-form;
(v) to compile machine-readable catalogue. The hard copies of it may be distributed among departmental libraries and other important resource centres;
(vi) to bring out list of current additions which may be circulated frequently; and
(vii) to provide computer search facilities for desired documents.

Departmental Reference Libraries for Government Documents

Each Ministry/Department should invariably have one library section which should be designated as depository library for all its published and unpublished documents. The functions of these libraries should be similar to the National Reference Library but limited to the ministry's publications. Its additional responsibility would be to provide one copy each of the ministry's document to the National Reference Library for Government Documents.

Depository Centres

There are a number of university libraries in India. In the initial stages all these libraries and those research institutes which are fully financed by the Government of India should be declared as depository libraries for government documents. After review of their functioning, more research libraries can be declared as depository centres. The maximum number by the end of the Eighth Five Year Plan should be not less than 500; in USA under the Depository Law of 1962, the maximum number of such libraries has been projected at 1,341.

Indian Council of Social Science Research, New Delhi took up depository activities by setting up Inter-Library Resources Centre (ILRC) in collaboration with Jawaharlal Nehru University in 1973. ILRC invited libraries in Delhi to deposit on loan or gratis their less used serial material including government documents at this Centre. In this way ILRC had at one time collected a good number of government documents. However, faced with many hurdles – mainly bureaucratic – it has so far not at all succeeded in achieving its objectives.

Clearing House Centres

A large number of official documents are released every year. It is natural that it would not be possible for the libraries to keep permanently all the old files due to space problem as well as the diminishing utility of the material. But before the material is weeded out by any library, a list of this may be sent to the Clearing House Centre. A consolidated list with location sources should be regularly circulated among the selected number of research libraries. Any library which requires particular title(s) may contact the donor library. There should be about half a dozen such Clearing House Centres covering all the regions in the country.

ILRC at one time initiated clearing house work and advised libraries in Delhi to provide information about the material to be weeded out. Among the government departmental libraries, ILRC received weeded out collection from the Department of Labour Library, Ministry of Finance Library, Ministry of Defence Library and Controller of Publications. The availability of the material was intimated to the research institutes outside Delhi and on receipt of requests, the desired titles were despatched. The tempo of the activity, however, could not be sustained due to bureaucratic problems again. Nevertheless, the need for such activity put on a sound footing still remains.

Location Tools

The library catalogues and accession lists are important sources for locating the desired documents. Leaving aside those libraries, which regularly bring out accession lists, one has to go from one library to another for retrieving the official material. Union Catalogues of official documents can make the search quite easier. National Social Science Documentation Centre (NASSDOC) took up a lead in this direction. It compiled *Union Catalogue of Serial Publications* available in libraries throughout India, which also covered official documents of serial nature. Separate volumes for each State were compiled. For Delhi, two separate volumes covering Central Government and State Government Serial Publications available in the libraries were brought out. Rajeshwari Dutta has compiled *Union Catalogue of the Central Government of India Publications held by libraries in London, Oxford and Cambridge*. It covers serial and non-serial material. The catalogue for non-serial material is urgently required to be compiled in India. The proposed National Reference Library for Government Documents could take up this responsibility.

CICIL series has taken in hand publication of a *Union Catalogue of the Government of India Publications held by Libraries in Delhi*.

Research Facilities

The National Reference Library for Government Document and Departmental Reference Libraries could be responsible for providing efficient information services like bibliographical, documentary, information retrieval, photo-copying, etc., to the non-official researchers.

Marketing of Publications

Infrastructure

The marketing infrastructure can be (i) a fully centralised,

(ii) partially centralised, or (iii) fully decentralised one. The centralised structure has been set-up in Great Britain where H.M.S.O. is the sole agency for marketing of all official documents. Partially decentralised system is followed in the USA where Superintendent of Documents is the biggest agency for sale of publications, but distribution is also done (1) free by Library of Congress, (2) free and sale by the several executive agencies, (3) sale by the Clearing House for Federal Scientific and Technical Information, Department of Commerce, and (4) sale by the Photo Duplication Service, Publications Board Project of the Library of Congress.

In India we are broadly following the U.S. pattern. The Controller of Publications is the main agency for publication and distribution of official documents along with other departmental and statutory agencies.

Review Copies

It is a matter of great consternation that though a large number of publications of research value are brought out by the Controller of Publications and other agencies, only a few of them receive attention for review. The only possible reason can be that the review copies are not sent to the editors of academic journals and newspapers. Good review can attract more clientele. Publication agencies should think of distributing a good number of copies for this purpose. The reviews in the journals of library and information science would facilitate quick selection by the librarians.

Other Measures

(i) There should be greater advertisement of selective titles in the leading newspapers and journals of India, quoting also from reviews, if any, appearing in the journals;

(ii) More copies of catalogues be circulated among user institutions. The cumulated annual and quinquennial volumes should be brought out in time;

(iii) Administrative and accounting procedures be streamlined to cut delays;

(iv) The Controller of Publications should send one copy of all the documents to all the Depository Centres;

(v) If possible, ISBN numbers in place of present identification number be given to the publications to keep in line with the international practices;

(vi) Pricing and marketing of government publications should follow a reasonable commercial pattern so that booksellers may take interest in supplying and selling the publications;

(vii) Credit facilities to the research institutes should be provided; and

(viii) Arrangement may be made for reprinting important publications which are for a long time out of print.

Role of Universities and Organisations

Research organisations and universities can play an important role in the marketing of publications by acting as Sale and Returns Agents. The Review Committee of ICSSR had recommended :

> "To overcome difficulties experienced by social scientists in obtaining government publications, ICSSR should prepare a monthly list of all government publications and send it out to universities and other research institutions."

To implement this, a Sales Section was set-up in NASSDOC in 1974 which started sending lists of selected titles of government documents collected from various official catalogues to the research institutions. It invited them to place orders for the desired listed items or for any other Central Government document. Acting in the capacity of Sales and Return Agent of Controller of Publications, it acquired material and supplied these to the research institutes. It got a very good response from the institutions. ICSSR has encouraging experience about this. But once again the bureaucratic attitude made the going difficult and thus bogged this down. Nonetheless Publication Divisions of the Universities can shoulder the responsibility of meeting the demands of the clientele within their area. The commercial booksellers need profit motive to push up the sales, but no such motive is required for the research bodies

Conclusion

The Controller of Publications holds the key to better supply of government documents. But, unless it improves its functioning by adopting scientific management techniques aided by modern information technology, spectacular progress cannot be expected. It is a pity that while stocks worth crores of rupees remain unsold with the Controller of Publications those who need cannot procure them. Functioning of Depository Centres also depends upon quick supply of documents and dissemination of information about new releases by it. Research organisations should, therefore, cooperate with the Controller of Publications in its efforts by creating more demand for its publications through extensive display at their centres and partaking in marketing activities. Extra efforts will be needed in keeping track of unpublished documents. There is every likelihood of their being lost after some time if not recorded at the appropriate time and place. The generation centres will have to extend their cooperation in this. A fruitful coordination is thus needed among those who generate, store, disseminate and use information. All efforts should be made to take jointly effective measures towards optimum utilisation of this important source of information.

The main issues which require attention are:

(i) Improvement in marketing techniques;
(ii) Setting up of more resource centres like National Reference Library for Government Documents, Departmental Reference Libraries, Depository Centres and Clearing House Centres;
(iii) Compilation of Local Union Catalogues of Government of India Publications; and
(iv) Full Bibliographical Control through Parliament Library.

BACKGROUNDERS

Amrik Singh, 1982, Publishing in Public Sector, *In*: Anon, 1982, *Libraries and the Book Trade: Papers: All India Seminar, February 14, 1982, Pragati Maidan, New Delhi*, Indian Library Association, Delhi, p. 48-53.

Chartrand, R.L., 1982, The Role of Government in the Information Society, *Journal of Information Science* 5(4) December, p. 137-142.

Krishnamurti, C.S., 1965, Acquisition of Government Publications, *Library Herald* 8(1-2) April-July, p. 82-94.

Mohinder Singh, 1982, *Government of India Publications*, Budua's Press, New Delhi, 176 p.

Mohinder Singh, 1985, *State Governments Publications in India, 1947-1982*, Academic Publication, New Delhi, 659 p., 2 vols.

Schmeckebier, Laurence F. and Eastin, Roy B., 1969, *Government Publications and Their use*, 2nd rev edn., Brookings Institution, Washington, D.C., x, 502 p.

6

INDIAN PROFESSIONALS IN INFORMATICS AND LIBRARIANSHIP

Proem

"Human resources, not capital, not income, nor material resources constitute the ultimate basis for the wealth of nations", maintains Frederick H. Harbison in his report based on the Project of the Inter-University Study of Human Resources in National Development. This becomes evident when we look at T.W. Schultz's comment:

> "Suppose that by some miracle, India, or some other low income country, acquired overnight, as it were, a set of natural resources, equipment, and structures, including techniques of production comparable per person to ours (i.e., the United States) what could they do with them, given the existing skills and knowledge, of the people? Surely the imbalance between the stock of human and non-human capital would be tremendous."

Definitions

In order to facilitate understanding, certain related terms, even if not used in subsequent discussion, are defined below:

Population constitutes the number of people living in a given place at a given time.

Workers are those who produce or transform goods or provide services for their own consumption and for that of others.

Labour Force in its most generalised form is conceived as that portion of the population which is economically active.

Working Force is used by some scholars as equivalent to Labour Force. However, the term Working Force may conveniently be used to refer to the workers or the employed.

Manpower is a broader term than Working Force; it not only includes the latter but generally also includes the potential or maximum available Working Force which might come into being in accordance with economic, social or political considerations.

Human Capital, forms the inherited and acquired abilities of producers and consumers.

Human Resources: Population, when channelised and given a direction is manpower. Manpower equipped with skills and disciplined to creativity becomes human resource.

Human Resources Development is the process of increasing the knowledge, the skill and the capacities of all the people in a society.

Purpose-built

In overall context, an analysis of main trends, approaches, accomplishments, contemporary issues relating to Human Resources Development with reference to Library and Information Science (LIS) personnel in India is presented.

Major Developments in Modern LIS and its Practice

The following is a highly selective and very sketchy enumeration of the major developments; it does not pretend to be an exhaustive historical survey culminating in the advent of a modern LIS and its practice. Its aim is rather to emphasise some aspects of the recent history of our profession, which may closely affect the curricula for ET (Education and Training) of LIS (Library and Information Science) personnel.

Emergence of Modern Librarianship

Librarianship, in the sense of collecting and storing books, has been practised for many centuries, but only within the past 100 years has it begun to take on the real characteristics of a profession. Melvil Dewey is considered as the father of modern librarianship as it is and Dr. Ranganathan that of the Indian child.

By the end of the past century, the basic technology of librarianship was elevated by Dewey, Ranganathan and other eminent librarians.

Emergence of Information Profession

Manifold development of Science and Technology resulted in the division of labour in Research and Development (R & D).

Some of the basic features of scientific research are *invariability*, i.e., verifiable openness or being available to all those who can make use of it; *reliability*, i.e., inter and intra-relationship of subjects; *applicability* for material development; *growth*, i.e., capability of further extension of frontiers of knowledge. *Communication* is common to these features and information constitutes a vital input.

Information, because of its importance to national development, is considered a national resource. To make full use of this resource, it needs to be properly managed. It is an extension of the traditional library functions, with the collection emphasis moving from books and journals to articles, reports and other special materials. The services are geared to meet intensive individual and group information needs rather than general loan and reference needs. To succeed in this task, the intermediary must be resourceful, have sufficient subject background, understand the seeker/user and his needs, be well acquainted with all the sources of information, and skilled in various information processing techniques.

Emergence of LIS Education

Systematic and organized ET in LIS is a relatively recent development of the past two or three decades. ET of information specialists is organised and offered either independently or in conjunction with ET of librarians.

Emergence of Theoretical Investigations

Modern LI practice and the growing need for well-trained professionals soon required not only the elaboration of practical rules, methods and guidelines which explain how to work, but obviously generated the need for investigations into the theoretical aspects of LI work. Dr. S.R. Ranganathan contributed substantially to the recognition of LIS as a scientific discipline.

Extension of the Types of Documents Handled

There are a good number of documents, in addition to traditional documents which are to be handled by professionals.

Information Explosion

The information explosion is in a way some what the other name of document explosion. The never ending increase in the volume of published and unpublished information sources posed growing difficulties in the handling of the mass of literature for librarians, information specialists and their institutions. It has given birth to secondary sources and more recently to the application of modern electronic and reprographic technology for information handling.

Increasing Role of Consolidated Information

There has been spectacular increase in the publication of abstracting and indexing publications.

Emergence of Reprographic and Computer Technologies

Newly invented reprographic technologies have become current practices in the LIS profession. Due importance is given to the use of computer in LIS profession for storage and retrieval.

Changing Role of Librarian

The traditional image of the librarian has faded out. The new role of the service librarian is supplemented by the library technologist, information technologist and information specialist, whose main duty is to serve seeker/user communities. To justify his role, LIS professionals have to acquire requisite knowledge of LIS and practice.

Aims of Human Resource Development

Thus, the human resource development should aim (i) to develop professionals for assuming a broader role of providing effective information to seekers/users; (ii) to develop scientific outlook in their jobs; (iii) to impart knowledge, skills and attitudes to LIS personnel which would contribute to productive and development programmes through effective information handling techniques; (iv) to develop adequate staff; (v) to enhance the aspirations and capabilities of staff; (vi) to place staff where he/she is best required; (vii) to provide for in-service training; (viii) to facilitate healthy working conditions; and (ix) to create cordial staff relations.

Historical Background

The recognition of the vital role of libraries in the educational, scientific and socio-economic development of the country is said to be rather a recent phenomenon which came into existence during the past two to three decades. One may agree or disagree with this and "Be as it may" as they say. Educated and efficient library staff is required to run these centres. In India before 1930 there was hardly any university or training centre to educate library staff. Today we have several universities in the country which conduct study at post-graduate level, i.e., Bachelor's degree in Library and Information Science or Master's degree in Library and Information Science.

Somc universities enrol students for M.Phil programme and Ph.D degree also.

Library associations and Women's Polytechnics, etc., offer certificate and diploma courses contributing to human resource development. In addition to these universities and associations, the Documentation Research and Training Centre (DRTC), Bangalore, and Indian National Scientific Documentation Centre (INSDOC), New Delhi, National Social Science Documentation Centre (NASSDOC) also offer training courses in documentation and/or information science.

The vast expansion of library and information science education in the country after Independence has naturally raised numerous problems which have been talked about in library committees, seminars, conferences and workshops.

As indicated above, library education imparted to professionals and semi-professionals becomes an important considerations for the success of library organisation in India.

LIS Education

Rapid expansion of library and information science in India after Independence raises questions about:

(i) Levels of education;
(ii) Vigorous selection at admission stage;
(iii) Richer curriculum;

(iv) Strengthening of faculty;
(v) Continuing education for the teachers;
(vi) Suitable aids in teaching;
(vii) Production of library science literature; and
(viii) Employment openings.

The Advisory Committee for Libraries appointed by the Government of India in its *Report* (1958, 1960) made several important recommendations. However, the *Report of UGC Review Committee* (1965) can rightly be considered as the first comprehensive document on the subject.

In addition, UGC has appointed a Panel of Library and Information Science to review periodically different aspects of the existing LIS education programmes in the country and make recommendations for future developments.

The recommendations of the UGC Panel with regard to various aspects such as status of library schools, teaching faculty, financial support, physical facilities, syllabi for BLIS, MLIS, M.Phil programme, etc., are already there with the library schools in the country for implementation.

Suggested Pattern

1. Duration of the Education and Training course at BLIS should be extended;
2. Dissertation writing should be made a compulsory paper at post-graduate level;
3. Introductory course of library science should be provided at under-graduate level;
4. Post-graduate course in library science should be designed as an advance course of two years' duration;
5. Research undertaken at Doctorate level should be either fundamental or problem oriented (oft-recurring problems);
6. In-service training and refresher courses should be given due importance;
7. Proper coordination between library science education in different universities in India should be made applicable;
8. Training of computer technology should be undertaken;
9. Application of audio-visual aids in teaching should be available; and
10. Introduction of library science education by open universities should be expanded.

Trends are not all that encouraging. Normally manpower resources do create bottlenecks. But in the case of LIS it is not entirely so, if the past experience, achievements and performance of libraries are any indication. As had often been felt in this context, an awareness of the problems, approaches used in alleviating them, accomplishment, and contemporary issues in the context of human resources development is generally lacking in our country. The LIS profession has so far received only lip sympathy from those who matter. In this context I recollect and reproduce what George Gissing has said:

> "It is because nations tend to stupidity and baseness that mankind moves so slowly; it is because individuals have a capacity for better things that it moves at all".

This aptly applies to Human Resources Development with particular reference to LIS Professionals. Administrators are generally too pre-occupied to pay heed to what human resources development concepts entail. Even intellectuals and professionals, when they happen to be at the decision-making level, neglect, rather tend to dismantle, whatsoever infrastructure is there, just for the sake of immediate short-term benefits and administrative convenience; and this, despite sufficient realisation that decision-making should be done on the basis of proven result. For human resources in Library Science and Informatics, extensive linking of would-be professionals with those at decision-making level is, therefore, a pre-requisite.

BACKGROUNDERS

Agrawal, S.P. and Satya Prakash, 1970, *Manpower Demand : Concepts and Methodology*, Meenakshi, Meerut, xvii, 368p.

Biscoe, E.L. and Ston, E.W., 1980, Motivation and Staff Development, *Journal of Library Education* 1(1), p 55-71.

Braunagel, J.S., 1979, Job Mobility of Men and Women Librarians and How it Effects Career Advancement, *American Libraries*, 10, p 643-647.

Elliott, Lynn, 1983, Professional Staff Development in Academic Libraries, *Journal of Librarianship* 15(4), p 237-253.

Mangla, P.B., 1981, Manpower Development for Information Handling, *Journal of Library and Information Science* 6(1), p 29-44.

Moore, N.E., 1980, *Manpower Planning in Libraries*, Library Association, London, 32p.

Rao, V.K.R.V., 1970, *Education and Human Resource Development*, Allied, Bombay, 231p.

7

INDIAN SOCIAL SCIENCE RESEARCH INSTITUTIONS

Genesis

Social Sciences in India are of recent origin. Their growth and development, which is a post-war phenomenon, is of great significance and importance, particularly in the developing countries. There is a virtual 'explosion' of social sciences in India and as a consequence of this 'explosion', there is general awareness, acceptance and use by the common laity, organizations — governmental and otherwise, scholars and researchers, business and industry and so on. In fact, there is hardly a social, economic or political problem that social scientists are not required to study and provide solution thereof. Social scientists help elevate such problems through a scientific social scrutiny and evaluation, particularly in industrially developed countries. The social sciences have, therefore, become an indispensable source of guidance for administrators and professionals of all kinds. They enlighten the people on the progress of ideas and make them see things through a wider perspective. If people today perceive the problems and their solution differently, it is because they are exposed to the perspective of social sciences — they raise their children differently, they have changed attitudes towards their governments, friends, neighbours and family members. Social Sciences influence the assumptions on which their daily lives are based. They contribute to rational thinking, a secular outlook, free from the "disenchantment of the world", which people weave around themselves.

Expansion of the social sciences, availability of funds and opportunity of participation in large-scale empirical study and research have placed a heavy responsibility on social scientists today. The Indian Council of Social Science Research (ICSSR), a pioneer organization in the field of social sciences in India, has provided financial assistance to social science institutions and has brought out a number of papers dealing with social science research in India. Naturally, therefore, social scientists will profit by keeping themselves abreast of new ideas and developments.

Historical Perspective

There has been, of late, a rapid growth of social science research and training organizations in the country. A host of research organizations have come into existence outside the university system and are playing an important and significant role in the developmental activities. There utility is being gradually realised and recognised with the progress and development of social science subjects. It is estimated that a large number of them are functioning as autonomous bodies, some receiving partial assistance, some full assistance, and some getting no financial support from the Government.

The first two research institutions, outside the university system, for purpose of research, teaching, training and policy formulation were formed as early as 1927 — one of them working in the field of Public Administration (All India Institute of Local-Self Government, Bombay) and the other had an inter-disciplinary character (Indian Council for Africa, New Delhi). In 1935 two more social science research organizations came to be set-up — one for Economics and the other for Statistics. Then came institutions in Political Science (1943), Anthropology (1945), Commerce (1946), Psychology (1949), Management (1949), Demography (1956), Law (1959), Criminology (1961) and Defence Studies (1965). A good number of them are multidisciplinary in their composition while others are department-based or are inter-disciplinary in their concern and approach. In addition to conducting research in various fields, they also function as training institutions for future researchers and administrators.

According to a list compiled by ICSSR in 1971, there were 59 professional social science associations in India. The largest number of associations was in the field of geography (10), followed by Anthropology (8) and Economics (7).

The first professional association was set-up in the year 1919 in History, followed by Anthropology, (1921), Geography (1926), Linguistics (1928), and Economics (1929). By 1947 — the year when India attained freedom – there were 16 such organizations; in ten year's time, i.e., by 1957, their number rose to 25, and in the later decade, ending 1967, as many as 22 were further added. In 1970, the total number had reached 59.

Table 7.1 shows the growth of research institutions period-wise and Table 7.2 subject-wise distribution. The analysis is based on the data collected for UNESCO's DARE system from 178 institutions during 1982. This can therefore serve only as a sample survey of existing institutions in India.

TABLE 7.1: Period-wise Foundation of Research Institutions

Period	No. of Institutions
Up to 1900	8
1901-1910	1
1911-1920	1
1921-1930	9
1931-1940	2
1941-1950	13
1951-1960	36
1961-1970	49
1971-1980	54
1981	5
	178

TABLE 7.2: Discipline-wise Distribution of Institutions

Sl. No.	Discipline	No. of Institutions	Sl. No.	Discipline	No. of Institutions
1.	Accounting	1	13.	Business Management	1
2.	Administrative Reforms	1	14.	Children	1
3.	Adult Education	2	15.	Commerce	1
4.	Agricultural Economics	6	16.	Community Development	1
5.	Agriculture	2	17.	Comparative Law	1
6.	America (United States)	2	18.	Consumer Education	1
7.	Anthropology	3	19.	Criminology	3
8.	Archaeology	1	20.	Cultural Anthropology	3
9.	Asia	3	21.	Demography	4
10.	Assam	1	22.	Development	3
11.	Behavioural Sciences	1	23.	Ecology	1
12.	Business Administration	2			

(Contd.)

TABLE 7.2 *(Contd.)*

Sl. No.	Discipline	No. of Institutions	Sl. No.	Discipline	No. of Institutions
24.	Economics	8	60.	Peace Research	4
25.	Economic Development	2	61.	Planning	1
26.	Education	10	62.	Policy Making	1
27.	Employment	3	63.	Political Science	3
28.	Environmental Planning	1	64.	Political System	1
29.	Family	1	65.	Population	7
30.	Family Planning	2	66.	Productivity	1
31.	Family Welfare	1	67.	Psychology	6
32.	Gandhian	4	68.	Public Administration	2
33.	Geography	5	69.	Public Enterprises	1
34.	Government	1	70.	Regional Development	2
35.	Higher Education	5	71.	Regional Planning	1
36.	Housing	2	72.	Religion	1
37.	India	1	73.	Research and Development	1
38.	Indology	1			
39.	Industrial Development	1	74.	Rural Development	8
40.	Industrial Relations	1	75.	Rural Planning	1
41.	Industry	3	76.	Science	2
42.	Information Centres	17	77.	Social Change	2
43.	International Affairs	2	78.	Social Problems	1
44.	International Law	1	79.	Social Sciences	10
45.	Islam	1	80.	Social Welfare	13
46.	Labour	2	81.	Social Work	2
47.	Labour Relations	1	82.	Society	1
48.	Law	1	83.	Socio-Economic Development	1
49.	Local Government	1			
50.	Management	11	84.	Sociology	11
51.	Marketing	1	85.	Statistics	3
52.	Mass Communication	2	86.	Teaching	8
53.	Mental Health	2	87.	Tibet	2
54.	National Income	1	88.	Tribes	1
55.	Nepal	1	89.	Urban Sociology	1
56.	Nomadism	1	90.	Urbanization	1
57.	Non-Violence	2	91	Women	1
58.	Organization	1	92.	Youth	1
59.	Parliamentary System	2			

Broadly, the burden of assisting the social science research in India is shared by three important agencies — Government, Private Bodies and International Organizations. The Government's contribution is the highest, i.e., about 90 per cent. As against *ad hoc* financing, the proportion of regular grant-in-aid by the Government is also the highest. In other words, most of the social science research institutions in India receive their regular grants from the Government sources. However, the mode and procedure followed by each organisation vary from one another. For instance, the Central Government allocates block grants to autonomous bodies, which in turn, frame their own rules and procedures for distribution of money to institutions and individuals wishing to conduct research in any branch of social sciences. But the sum spent on social sciences is meagre as compared to what is spent on scientific and technological researches. According to an estimate, country is spending annually about Rs. 2500 million on research in natural, technological and medical sciences and around Rs. 25 million on research in social sciences. Similarly, the international organizations, which have large amounts, provide grants for social science research either directly to the Government or to research institutions after obtaining formal approval of the Government. Here too, the amount spent on social science research is small as compared to what is spent on scientific research.

The existing sources of financing social science research in India are within following sectors:

I. Public/Government Sector:
   (a) Ministries/Departments of Central and State Governments.
   (b) Autonomous Organisations, sponsored and funded by the Government.
   (c) National Banks and Public Financial Institutions.

II. Private Sector:
   (a) Private Research Institutions.
   (b) Professional Organisations.
   (c) Industrial Houses and Individual Companies.

III. International Sector:
   (a) National Organisations sponsoring and funding research activities in the third world countries.
   (b) International Organisations.

ICSSR conducted a study in respect of financing of social science research in India with the following objectives in view:

(a) to identify institutions and agencies financing the social science research;
(b) to quantify their financial inputs and assess their relative contribution;
(c) to analyse patterns and procedures of financing;
(d) to observe the nature of studies and researches emerging from the expenditure; and
(e) to make suggestions for coordinating the system of providing financial support.

The study covered all the three above funding sectors for the period from 1947-48 to 1977-78. Finding of the study are briefly given below:

Central/State Government Departments

The Government plays two distinct but related roles in the research sphere – those of sponsor and user. The impetus to planned economic growth has produced an awareness of and need for social science research and consequently government sponsored research is greatly devoted to socio-economic problems facing the country and is mostly of ad hoc nature.

The study identified 55 departments of the Central Government considered to be the possible agencies which could sponsor research and provide financial support to research organisations. The response received was encouraging. Among the Central Ministries, the following were found to be originator of large volume of research directly and indirectly by providing financial support to research undertaken by other institutions:

1. Ministry of Agriculture
2. Ministry of Finance
3. Ministry of Education and Social Welfare (*now* Ministry of Human Resource Development)
4. Ministry of Health
5. Ministry of Labour
6. Planning Commission

Autonomous Funding Organizations

The study identified undermentioned funding agencies. Information about their activities, aims and objectives, organizational structure, field of research (priorities), research policy, method of research promotion, finance, area of research, long-term plan, collaboration and coordination, research facilities available, seminar/workshops conducted, income and expenditure, procedure or making grants, etc., to social science research in India is provided in the study. Also provided are basic data about published and unpublished documents and other interesting features.

Funding Agencies

1. Central Social Welfare Board
2. Family Planning Foundation
3. Indian Council of Agricultural Research
4. Indian Council of Child Welfare
5. Indian Council of Cultural Relations
6. Indian Council of Historical Research
7. Indian Council of Medical Research
8. Indian Çouncil of Social Science Research
9. National Council of Applied Economic Research
10. National Council of Educational Research and Training
11. National Productivity Council
12. University Grants Commission

Banking Institutions

ICSSR as a part of its study approached 85 banking institutions including the Reserve Bank of India to collect information as to how far they have been able to equip themselves for the tasks assigned to them by undertaking or sponsoring research in various desired fields.

It was found that the research activities of banking institutions are problem oriented, i.e., of a functional character suiting the requirements of the concerned institutions. Their studies are short term surveys of a particular area or region and thus are of ad hoc rather than of a continuing nature. Reserve Bank of India and State Bank of India were found to be the leading institutions in social science research.

Industrial and Commercial Houses

Like the banking institutions, research projects of industrial and commercial houses were also of functional character, suiting to the requirement of the concerned industry, i.e., problem oriented and of an ad hoc nature.

International Agencies

ICSSR conducted a similar study in respect of financing of social science research in India by the 12 international organizations mentioned below:

1. American Institute of Indian Studies (AIIS)
2. British Council Division
3. Food and Agricultural Organisation of the United Nations (FAO)
4. Ford Foundation
5. International Labour Organization (ILO)
6. Shastri Indo-Canadian Institute
7. United Nations Children's Emergency Fund (UNICEF)
8. United Nations Development Programme (UNDP)
9. United States Educational Foundation in India (USEFI)
10. United Nations Educational, Scientific and Cultural Organization (UNESCO)
11. World Bank
12. World Health Organisation (WHO)

The main objectives of the study were (i) to identify international agencies, which directly undertake or provide financial assistance for social science research in India, (ii) to quantify the financial inputs provided for the purpose, and (iii) to analyse the patterns and procedures adopted by the various foreign funding agencies for providing financial support for social science research. These agencies were approached to supply the requisite information on a set pattern, laid down in a questionnaire, as in the case of other studies about their basic objectives, research programmes and other facilities available with them.

It may thus be seen that there exist a number of agencies financing the social science research in the country. However, lack of coordination among the funding agencies created problems – on one hand of duplication of research and on the other imbalanced research in the different branches of social sciences. Moreover, research output by various research institutions is not fully utilised. Realising the need for a comprehensive information system for utilisation of research, ICSSR brought out two directories of social science research institutions and professional organisations in India in 1971-72. These directories soon became out of date as a large number of institutions came into being. In addition, the nature and type of research activities, administrative and financial management also underwent a considerable change.

As a part of its larger study — the financing of social science research in India – ICSSR collected useful data about research institutions in India. This resulted in compilation of updated *Directory of Research Institutions and Professional Organisations in India* in mimeographed form in 1981. Most of the research institutions or organisations listed in the *Directory* are outside the university system but university institutions of national importance have been included in it. Information about each institution includes: Name and Address, Year of Establishment, Status, Executive Head, History, Structure, Aims and Field of Research, Staff, Research Facilities, Data Processing Equipment, Training Programmes, Finance, Research project and publications. Arrangement of the entries is first statewise and within State alphabetical by their official names.

Quite separately, UNESCO collected information in respect of social science research institutions for input in the DARE System. In view of the considerations mentioned above, ICSSR accepted the responsibility to update information available in DARE print-outs. A preliminary list of research institutions and professional organisations was accordingly prepared out of the material available from a number of sources including particularly the two directories prepared by the ICSSR earlier and the DARE print-outs. A total of 405 institutions were identified. These included research institutions/ professional organisations in the field of social sciences which are set-up by Central/State Governments. Industrial and commercial houses and other private bodies were also included for the purpose of updating the information. Questionnaires were sent to all of them. A Statewise break-up of the institutions and professional organisations is given in the Table 7.3.

TABLE 7.3: State-wise Distribution of Institutions

Sl. No.	Name of the State/ Union Territory	No. of Institutions	Sl. No.	Name of the State/ Union/Territory	No. of Institutions
1.	Andhra Pradesh	27	13.	Maharashtra	60
2.	Arunachal Pradesh	2	14.	Manipur	1
3.	Assam	7	15.	Meghalaya	1
4.	Bihar	12	16.	Mizoram	1
5.	Chandigarh	1	17.	Nagaland	2
6.	Delhi	78	18.	Orissa	7
7.	Gujarat	27	19.	Punjab	3
8.	Himachal Pradesh	3	20.	Rajasthan	18
9.	Jammu and Kashmir	3	21.	Sikkim	2
10.	Karnataka	20	22.	Tamil Nadu	29
11.	Kerala	14	23.	Uttar Pradesh	35
12.	Madhya Pradesh	7	24.	West Bengal	45
				Total	405

The updated DARE print-outs, quite obviously, provide the useful basic information to the research scholars in social sciences about various research institutions and organisations, thus enabling optimum utilisation of facilities available with these research agencies on the one hand, and on the other help research agencies to have an idea of the researches undertaken or completed and facilities provided by other similar bodies to build close links for the promotion of social science research and its utilisation.

India has had a haphazard growth of social science institutions, but the situation has been improving. New institutions, including professional organisations have started coming up. Now it would be necessary not only to speed them up, but to make sure that their growth is brought about in a coordinated manner. Establishment of ICSSR has filled the institutional gap which had stood for a long time in the way of the development of social science research in India and is a source for regular supply of finance to research institutions enabling them to plan their research work well ahead.

PART IV

LINKAGES

8

INDIAN NATIONAL NETWORK FOR SOCIAL SCIENCE INFORMATION AND DOCUMENTATION CENTRES (INSIDOC)

(Proposed)

Information as a resource has become a key factor in the socio-economic development of the countries and the degree of its effective utilisation distinguishes the highly developed societies of the world from those that are still developing.

Development is a very complex and multi-dimensional process involving information and knowledge inputs of scientific and technological research and their applications, dovetailed with other societal information such as political, economic, demographic, health, etc. The developing countries have to accept this fact. The earlier these countries, individually and in unison, make effort to plan for optimum utilisation of this important resource, the sooner they could hope to achieve their long-cherished objectives of removing poverty and illiteracy as also that of developing self-reliant economy.

Asia-Pacific Information Network in Social Sciences (APINESS) launched on 12-16 May 1986, is laudable as it would facilitate exchange of experiences and sharing of resources and facilities for tackling socio-economic issues which are mostly common to all the countries of the region. The achievement in this area will usher in a new international socio-economic order, which would ensure their sovereignty along with international peace and security.

The successful functioning of regional networking quite naturally would depend upon the efficient system of national networks and, within that, the local networks. This would require survey of present-day activities and existing resources — human and physical — to be strengthened, rationalised, and coordinated, creating new capabilities and facilities

The structural/institutional framework of national networks, to form part of APINESS or otherwise may be suggested as under:

NATIONAL NODE

The National Social Science Documentation Centre (NASSDOC) in the Indian Council of Social Science Research could be the National Focal Point or National Node for the regional network as it has the necessary resources, infrastructure and programmes to carry out the functions expected of a Node. The financial resources of NASSDOC are being met by ICSSR. The existing infrastructure includes documentation units at six ICSSR regional centres (Appendix-8), mostly located in university campuses at Bombay, Calcutta, Chandigarh, Delhi, Hyderabad and Shillong, twenty four ICSSR financed leading social science research institutes and other cooperating libraries/institutions. The documentation and data services programmes include providing financial assistance for (a) documentation and data archives projects, (b) holding of professional seminars, conferences and training programmes, (c) strengthening documentary and data resources in the research institutions, (d) promoting networking activities, among documentations and data centres, and (e) publication of documents on library and information science and data management.

NASSDOC in association with ICSSR Data Archives is thus capable to act as a National Node, i.e., to take up responsibility to promote the concept of network and to coordinate, encourage and monitor the progress of national networking. Both NASSDOC and ICSSR Data Archives are at an advanced stage of providing documentation and data services and have already taken up a number of programmes to encourage resource sharing and networking. Some of the activities are as under:

Networking/Resources Sharing Activities

(i) Compilation of Union Catalogue of Serial/Periodicals of Libraries in India, 32 vols, 1972-76;
(ii) Compilation of Union List of Current Periodicals being Received in Delhi, revised in 1985;
(iii) Retrospective indexing of about 240 Indian social science periodicals from their inception to the year 1970 (in progress);

(iv) Compilation of bibliographies on the States/Union Territories of India (in progress);
(v) Compilation of bibliographies of social science research material in the regional languages of India including English (in progress);
(vi) Setting up of Inter-Library Resources Centre at Delhi in 1976 in collaboration with Jawaharlal Nehru University, inviting libraries to deposit their less used serial material at the Centre. Thirty libraries deposited about 1 lakh volumes of periodicals; ILRC, however is now almost non-functional;
(vii) Acquisition of unpublished PhD. theses in social sciences approved by Indian universities. It could become the largest centre of this grey material throughout India (collection at present: more than 2500);
(viii) Provision of bibliographic services to the scholars;
(ix) Acting as input centre for Indian material for ICSSID International Bibliographies; International Bulletin of Bibliography on Education (BIBE Project, Madrid); International Geographical Bibliography (Paris). Also updated information on behalf of UNESCO Social Science Documentation Centre, Paris in respect of research institutions and periodicals in social sciences in India for DARE DATA BANK;
(x) Exchange agreements with well over 2000 Indian and foreign institutions for exchange of publications;
(xi) Inter-library loan facilities; and
(xii) Consultancy services in respect of setting up of documentation units and Data centres.

Proposed New Activities

(i) Central abstracting of social science literature produced in India;
(ii) Compilation of South Asia Index;
(iii) Continuing education programme leading to Associateship in Library and Information Studies in Social Sciences.

Networking Associate Programmes

NASSDOC has been developing close relations with international library and documentation organisations to promote the networking concept. The Director (NASSDOC) was a member of the National Committee of International Federation for Information and Documentation (FID) to pursue collaborative documentation programmes in the region.

NASSDOC has also developed relations with the International Federation of Library Associations and Institutions (IFLA).

Besides exchange relations with international organisations, NASSDOC has similar relations with a large number of institutions all over the world. Selective list of institutions in Asia and the Pacific region is given in the Appendix-VII to indicate close relations already achieved for mutual benefit and the potential for further links in networking.

Data Archives Networking/Resource Sharing Activities

(i) Compilation of an inventory of data generated by different research institutions in India since 1951;
(ii) Developing general purpose application programmes for statistical processing for research scholars and institutions;
(iii) Serving as Regional Secretariat of the International Association for Social Science Information Service and Technology. A plan for exchange of data and software with other archives in India and abroad is on the planning board; and
(iv) Compilation of *National Register of Social Scientists in India,* which covers more than 7,500 scholars working in the university departments, colleges and research institutes. The whole data has been computerised.

SPECIALISED CENTRES

There are a number of specialised centres – discipline-oriented and mission-oriented – in India. Their participation on a voluntary basis in the network would ensure its successful functioning.

As most of the countries in the region are giving priority to solving issues of socio-economic nature, it would be appropriate to identify networking potentialities in the above field and in the first stage enlist libraries and information centres specialising in development research literature for networking.

The resources of some lead centres, supplemented by a list of few others, arranged under sub-discipline, is given below to explore their willingness to participate in the network.

Lead Centres

Centre for Development and Instructional Technology (CENDIT). New Delhi (1972)

Specialises in education, development and communication technology subjects. It has holdings of 3,700 books and 1,237 microfilms, 10,000 product literature and data bases on magnetic tapes. It is the input centre for documents produced in India for DEVSIS data base. Compiles *Devindex India.* It has installed ISIS package.

Centre on Rural Documentation (CORD), Hyderabad (1958)

Specialises in development sciences. Holds 45,000 books and bound periodicals and 10,000 reports. Provides reprography, translation and audio-visual facilities. Compiles *CORD Index* (Monthly) and *CORD Abstracts* (Bi-Monthly). The index covers 600 journals and 13 newspapers. The indexing slant is towards policy-making.

Giri Institute of Development Studies, Lucknow (1973)

Library specialises in development sciences literature which includes Government reports and World Bank publications. It has computer facilities.

Gokhale Institute of Politics and Economics, Pune (1930)

Library specialises in the disciplines of Economics, Sociology, Statistics and Political Science. Holds about 200,000 books and 1,000 microforms. Dipository Centre for UN publications and special collection includes British Parliamentary papers and government documents of the USA and Commonwealth countries. Provides reprography and translation services. Brings out *List of additions* and *Fortnightly list of articles on India.*

Indian Council of World Affairs, New Delhi (1944)

Specialises in the disciplines of International Affairs, International Law and Economics. Holdings include 110,000 books and 11,500 microfilms. Special collection includes press clippings and UN documents. Compiles *Weekly List of Articles and Documenta-*

tion on Asia.

Indian Institute of Foreign Trade, New Delhi (1964)
Library specialises in trade literature. Holdings include 50,000 books and about 5,000 documents. Brings out *Documentation on Foreign Trade.*

Indian Statistical Institute, Calcutta, (1931)
Library specialises in literature in Statistics, Computer Science, Economics, etc. Holdings include about 200,000 books and periodicals, 375,000 maps and 3,500 microforms. Provides current awareness services, bibliographical services and SDI services.

Institute of Applied Manpower Research, New Delhi, (1962)
Library's subject specialisation is Manpower, Economics, Statistics and Management. Holdings include 14,000 books and 15,000 bound periodical volumes. Brings out *List of Additions* and *Manpower Documentation.*

Institute of Public Enterprise, Hyderabad, (1964)
Library's subject specialisation is Public Enterprise Studies, Policy Studies and Management. Special collection includes annual reports of State and Central Government public undertakings. Brings out *List of Additions* and *List of Parliamentary Reports.* Compiles *Annotated Bibliography of Public Enterprises.*

National Council of Applied Economic Research, New Delhi (1956)
Library's specialised literature covers Economics, Agriculture, Transportation and Energy. Collection include 18,147 books, 20,938 reports and 1,053 microforms. Brings out *Artha Suchi: Index of Indian Economic Literature* on HP 3,000 computer, using MINISIS software package. Besides this, compiles topical bibliographies.

National Informatics Centre (NIC), New Delhi (1977)
Specialises in developing interactive data bases in network of computers for the Government of India and State Governments. In the field of documentation NIC has undertaken development of the bibliographic system on techno-economic information documents. It developed a Pilot System for the National Medical

Library for providing medical retrieval service, and Legal Information Retrieval System, based on the Constitution of India for the Ministry of Law, Justice and Company Affairs in 1984. Provides online bibliographic service for documents in the library and for news-items on electronics and computers. Brings out *Weekly Current News Update.* MINISIS Application Package is used for bibliographic services.

Parliament Library, New Delhi (1921)

Holdings contain 500,000 books consisting of Central, State and Foreign Government reports, UN and allied agencies publications and Gazettes, Debates, Acts, Rules, etc. Documentation activities cover compilation of *Journal of Parliamentary Information, Abstracts and Index of Reports* and *Digest of Legislative and Constitutional Cases.* Brings out topical bibliographies.

Planning Commission, New Delhi (1950)

Library holdings include 150,000 books; periodical subscription is 800; special collection consists of 5,000 pamphlets, 10,000 plans and 1,000 maps. Compiles indexing and abstracting periodical *Doc-Plan* and a list of *Recent Additions to the Library.*

Regional Information Centre for Development Policy Modelling, Pune, (1984)

Specialises in economic modelling to help policy-makers to choose a suitable one. Present collection includes 2,000 documents. The Centre has computer facilities and proposes to automate library procedures. The Centre works as a regional focal point for modelling in Asia.

Research and Information System for the Non-Aligned and Other Developing Countries (RISNODEC), New Delhi, (1984)

Set-up on the recommendation of NAM countries in their meeting at New Delhi. Priority research areas are (a) wage and payments problems of the developing countries, (b) money and finance issues, and (c) analytical digest of current trends in the world economy. On the documentation side, networking with other research institutions, government departments and UN bodies is contemplated. Compiled *Directory of Research Institutes/Information System.* The institution has computer facilities.

Small Enterprises National Documentation Centre (SENDOC), Hyderabad, (1970)

Provides comprehensive technical, economic and financial management information services to small industries. Special collection includes 5,000 produce profiles and 5,000 trade catalogues. Brings out *SENDOC Chronicle, SENDOC Bulletin* and *Appropriate Technology Documentation Bulletin.* Conducts short-term training courses in information storage and retrieval systems.

Tata Institute of Social Sciences, Bombay, (1930)

Library's specialised disciplines include Social Work, Personnel Management, Rural and Urban Development, etc. Holdings consist of 58,000 books, 2,000 pamphlets and 500 reprints. Brings out monthly *Documentation list.*

See also Appendix-II

Supporting Centres

Agriculture

Indian Agricultural Research Institute Library, New Delhi.
Indian Council of Agricultural Research Library, New Delhi.
Indian Society of Agricultural Economics Library, Bombay.

Cooperation

National Cooperative Development Corporation Library, New Delhi.
National Cooperative Union of India Library, New Delhi.
National Institute of Public Cooperation and Child Development Library, New Delhi.
Vaikunth Mehta National Institute of Cooperative Management Library, Pune.

Demography

International Institute for Population Studies Library, Bombay.

Foreign Trade and Investment

Indian Investment Centre Library, New Delhi.
Indian Council for Research on International Economic Relations Library, New Delhi.

Human Resources

Centre for Human Development and Social Change Library, Madras.
Centre for Women Development Studies Library, New Delhi.
Labour Bureau Library, Shimla.
Labour Documents and Reference Centre, New Delhi.
National Labour Institute Library, New Delhi.
Sri Ram Centre for Industrial Relations and Human Resources Library, New Delhi.
Xavier Labour Relations Institute Library, Jamshedpur.

Industries

Bureau of Public Enterprises Library, New Delhi.
Centre for Studies in Decentralised Industries Library, Bombay.
Institute of Public Enterprise, Hyderabad.
Small Industries Extension Training Institute Library, Hyderabad.

Rural Development

Centre for Research in Rural and Industrial Development, Chandigarh.
Ministry of Rural Development Library, New Delhi.
Rural Institute Library, Amravati.
Rural Institute, Gandhiji-Lincoln Library, Gandhigram.
State Training Institute of Community Development Library, Bhubaneshwar.

Socio-economic Development

A.N. Sinha Institute of Social Studies Library, Patna.
Centre for Economic and Social Studies Library, Hyderabad.
Centre for Development Studies Library, Trivandrum.

Centre for Policy Research Library, New Delhi.
Centre for Regional, Ecological and Science Studies in Development Alternatives, Calcutta.
Centre for Research in Rural and Industrial Development, Chandigarh.
Centre for Social Studies Library, Surat.
Centre for Studies in Social Sciences Library, Calcutta.
Centre for Study of Developing Societies Library, New Delhi.
Council for Social Development Library, New Delhi.
Delhi School of Economics Library, New Delhi.
Delhi School of Social Work Library, Delhi.
G.B. Pant Social Science Institute Library, Allahabad.
Gandhian Institute of Studies Library, Varanasi.
Gujarat Institute of Area Planning, Ahmedabad.
Indian Institute of Economics Library, Hyderabad.
Indian Social Institute Library, New Delhi.
Institute for Social and Economic Change Library, Bangalore.
Institute of Development Studies Library, Jaipur.
Institute of Economic Growth Library, Delhi.
Institute for Studies in Industrial Development, New Delhi.
L.N. Mishra Institute of Economic Development and Social Change Library, Patna.
Madras Institute of Development Studies, Madras.
Ministry of Finance Library, New Delhi.
National Institute of Public Finance and Policy Library, New Delhi.
National Institute of Social Defence Library, New Delhi.
Sardar Patel Institute of Economic and Social Research Library, Ahmedabad.

Statistics

Census Operations Library, Madras.
Central Statistical Organisation Library, New Delhi.
Indian Statistical Institute Library, New Delhi.
See also Appendix-I

ADMINISTRATION

ICSSR has set-up Committees, viz., Committee on Documentation Services and Research Information, Committee on Data Archives, and Committee on Training, etc., to advise and recommend programmes for documentation and data services. All these Committees consist of professional experts and renowned social scientists in India.

The infrastructure for National Network Advisory Committee thus exists. It may consist of members from these committees and representatives from participating institutions.

The secretariat may be located at NASSDOC-ICSSR, New Delhi.

ACTIVITIES

Priority could be given to the following activities:

Training Programmes

The impact of information technology has forced librarians to think of new information management techniques. The professionals at managerial level need introduction to mechanised methods of management for creating efficient system for storage, retrieval and dissemination of information. Library training programmes, covering the above aspects, have become more urgent. These would help in better management of network activities too.

Keeping in view the need for the above, NASSDOC could undertake library courses which could lead to Associateship in Library and Information Studies in Social Sciences for professionals at managerial level. Concurrent with this, short-term courses under Continuing Education Programme, which were conducted to begin with, should continue.

Inventory of Documentation Resources

Most of the libraries and information centres bring out indexing and abstracting journals without any coordination and standardisation. This results, on the one hand, in overlapping in coverage leading to wastage of money and manpower, and on the other, leaving some disciplines uncovered.

The documentation lists in existence may, therefore, be identified. Their coverage, presentation pattern and financial sources may be looked into. Lead libraries may be assigned responsibility of bringing out indexing and/or abstracting journals in their respective fields. International standards for compiling documents will have to be followed in order to facilitate exchange among network members. Priority could be given to compilation of data in machine-readable form. A priliminary listing of Documentation Resources is given in Appendix-III.

Bibliographical Control of Non-Doctoral Research (in Progress and Completed)

A large number of developmental research programmes are under way in India. To avoid duplication and to have optimum use of the information created, the bibliographical control of research is very essential. Networking partners will have to join hands for this, obviously not overlooking international standards for compiling such tools.

Incidentally, NASSDOC has been bringing out documents covering ICSSR financed research project (completed and in progress), and also the projects undertaken by ICSSR financed research institutes. These documents require to be revised and updated according to international bibliographic standards, and further the data is to be computerised for exchange and online services.

Directory of Research Institutions

Directories of above nature are available – reference can be made to those brought out by NASSDOC-ICSSR – but these require to be updated and standardised.

Union Catalogue of Books and Union Catalogue of Periodicals/Serials

The *Union Catalogue of Social Sciences Periodicals/Serials* has been compiled by NASSDOC, covering material available in libraries up to 1972. The catalogue requires to be updated and computerised. Further, steps to bring out discipline-oriented union catalogues should be undertaken.

CICIL series includes a union catalogue of *Communication, Informatics and Librarianship* publications in Delhi Libraries, and plans to have in the net more disciplines.

Exchange of Professionals

A system is required to be devised for exchange of professionals as partners in the network, to observe functioning of national networks in other countries of the region. This will facilitate personal contact for exchange of experiences and will develop close affinity between them.

FINANCIAL SUPPORT

Financial support is required for providing micro-computer system to Lead Centres which, in the initial stages, may not be more than ten. The compilation of different tools for resource sharing will also require initial investment. The other items of expenditure will include training programmes, exchange of personnel and subscription to foreign data bases. The approximate budget as per statement in Table 8.1 will come to Rs. 140.00 lakhs. The expenditure can be spread over three years.

TABLE 8.1: Estimated Expenditure (Spread over Three Years)

Item	User Centres	Application	Amount Rs. (in lakhs)
1. Main-frame Computer	National Focal Node	Centralised storing of data relevant to (a) Union Catalogue (b) Indexing and Abstracting Services (c) Directory of Research in progress and completed (d) Directory of Research Institutions (e) Inventory of Data Sets	50.00
2. Micro-computers	Specialised Centres (10)	(a) Creation of data bases (b) SDI Services (c) Online searches of existing data bases within and outside the region	40.00

Contd.

	Item	User Centres	Application	Amount Rs. (in lakhs)
3.	Initial Investment in Creation of Data Bases			20.00
4.	Training Programmes	National Focal Node	Holding of workshops within the region	10.00
5.	Exchange of Personnel		To exchange experiences and first-hand observations of working of existing networks	10.00
6.	Subscription to Foreign Data Bases	National Focal Node and Specialised Centres	SDI Services	10.00
			Total: Rs.	140.00

9

INDIAN NATIONAL INFORMATION SYSTEM FOR SOCIAL SCIENCES (INISS)

(Proposed)

Introduction

Information is now regarded as a vital national resource to be developed and made available to all those who need it. It is increasingly being realised that development of capability in information handling and dissemination would help a country in knowledge advancement, understanding, decision-making, techno- logy transfer, minimising duplication of efforts, conservation of resources, etc. The idea is gaining ground that the social and economic system of a country would function more efficiently, if availability of reliable information is ensured at the right time. Information—an intellectual resource as well as most valuable of all resources—is becoming the essential basis for the maintenance of modern society at whatever stage of development it may be. Most countries recognise today that better information services help to achieve a progressive society. These countries have, therefore, started examining the need for systematic planning of their present information infrastructure so as to utilise fully the information accumulated at the national level and to be able to participate in and benefit from existing and future world information systems in various fields of activity.

In India, information systems, services and facilities are being built up at various levels. It becomes necessary to work towards a general plan in agreement with all the principal information agencies so as to ensure that the world's specialised and professional knowledge is fully and properly used in guiding social evolution. The government, on its part, should be aware of the need for integrating the elements of information infrastructure in the overall development plans. The basic plan of action is to build an information network on the existing infrastructure by coordinating the present activities, articulating the various services, developing their strong points, encouraging private and public initiatives and filling in existing gaps.

India has made appreciable progress in the development of information facilities. The Government's support and assistance in building up information capability are quite evident. In the field of science and technology, the National Information System for Science and Technology (NISSAT) has already been ushered in. National Informatics Centre has also been developed to handle data required for planning and decision-making by the government agencies. National Technical Manpower Information System (NTMIS), Urban and Regional Information System (URIS), Corporate Information System (CIS) as also agriculture, medical and trade information systems are being implemented. Social science research in India has gained momentum after the establishment of the Indian Council of Social Science Research (ICSSR). ICSSR, even in its first year of establishment, had thought it appropriate to set up a Documentation unit, later developed as National Social Science Documentation Centre (NASSDOC) to support the research and development efforts in social sciences. Later on, the Council also established a Data Archives for social sciences. NASSDOC successfully completed its development phase poising to step up its activities and to take up new programmes. Along side with the further development of NASSDOC, efforts have to be made to conceive of Indian National Information System for Social Sciences (INISS). In the field of social sciences, a number of libraries and information centres with differing functions, scope and efficiency have come into being under the auspices of academic institutions, research institutions, government departments, etc. In a stage of development, these libraries and information centres have sprung up piecemeal without liaison between them, without plan and without cooperation. It is necessary at this stage, therefore, to coordinate or marshal such a large number of centres of information services into a well-structured national information system/network. The impetus for an information network arises out of economic and time pressures which force organisations to share rather than duplicate information resources and facilities. The national system is not something new. It would be based on existing information facilities. It would make full use of the information potential of the country by coordinating the activities and by seeking the cooperation of individual information centres, according to well-defined guidelines and division of responsibilities. It may fill the existing lacunae in information services by establishing new ones. It may develop and apply compatible national standards for information techniques and methods to facilitate interchange of information and also introduce modern methods of information handling.

Planning Guidelines

In developing a national system, it becomes necessary to work towards a general plan, in agreement with main information agencies, indicating the allocation of responsibility and the means it intends to employ such as specialised services, incentives, coordinating machinery, financial arrangements, etc. A framework reflecting the needs of all sectors of national endeavours is necessary to guide the establishment of a national information system.

The Social Scientists as well as Information Scientists are increasingly aware of the importance of the Documentation services and those supported by Data Archives. And as such steps have to be taken to set-up separately, Data Archives Units and Documentation Units. What, therefore, follows applies equally to Documentation services and Data Archives services as an integral part of Information services. The structure of a Indian National Information System for Social Sciences (INISS), quite obviously, will have the following main components:

1. Documentation and Library Services
2. Data Archives Services

To be effective, both these services are required to develop somewhat simultaneously in the vertical as well as horizontal planes.

In the matter of information resource development, guidelines are required with reference to:

(a) allocation of responsibilities to institutions for building up strong collections in special fields,
(b) ensuring that there is in the country at least one accessible copy of every worthwhile publication for use by scholars,
(c) provision of a national lending library service,
(d) establishment of a data bank for socio-economic data,

(e) preparation of national union catalogues of holdings of libraries, and
(f) establishment of regional dormitories for storing older, but important for research, material weeded out by service libraries.

As regards information seekers/users, the guidelines should cover:

(a) identifying the present and potential seekers/users of information and assessing their requirements,
(b) creation of information consciousness among seekers/users, and
(c) organising programmes for training of seekers/users of information.

The guidelines for offering information service should include:

(a) development of necessary tools, techniques and services adequate to meet seekers'/users' needs and demands, as these change from time to time at different levels,
(b) establishment of subject-oriented information grids,
(c) establishment of referral services,
(d) provision of translation facilities, and
(e) provision of adequate computer facilities for information retrieval.

The guidelines with reference to manpower development cover:

(a) building up of expertise and provision for education and training for an adequate number of professional personnel,
(b) supporting projects in information fields,
(c) supporting research programmes,
(d) sponsoring conferences, symposia, seminars, workshops, etc., and
(e) securing adequate service conditions and status for library and information science personnel.

There should also be guidelines regarding cooperation with other national and international organisations engaged in information and/or related type of services.

Objectives

The objectives of INISS may be stated in general terms as follows:

1. To facilitate the selection, processing and communication of ideas from the point of generation and availability to their potential seekers/users at all levels;
2. To ensure that the information made available is precise, exhaustive and accessible with a minimum delay, presented in a manner convenient to the seekers/users, and services provided at a reasonable cost;
3. To promote the development and use of efficient tools and techniques of information handling; and
4. To make optimum utilisation of existing information systems and services and development of new ones.

Pre-requisites

Essential pre-requisites for development of INISS, among others, are:

1. Government support and encouragement including formulation of policy for information;
2. Adequate manpower resources and potential for training manpower;
3. Information resources and facilities (data archives, libraries, specialised documentation and information centres);
4. Publication capabilities;
5. Computer and communication capabilities;
6. Reprography facilities;
7. Good organisational machinery; and
8. Standardisation in materials, techniques and patterns of service.

Status of Social Science Research in India

Social sciences as discipline of study and research have already made recognizable developments in India since Independence. They are already being taken notice of as a resource by the government and other public and private organisations in promoting economic development and social change. They have shown the capacity to grow and expand in terms of centres of teaching and research, manpower and professional organisations.

Although as compared to teaching and research in natural and applied sciences, social sciences have lagged behind in progress and financial support, their achievements and development during the past three decades are really encouraging. An idea about the present status of the social sciences in India can be obtained from a number of indicators, i.e., number of post-graduate departments; number of doctoral theses; number of students registered for PhD.; number of professional institutions; volume of publications; social science manpower, etc. Although updated current statistics about these indicators are not easily available, yet on the basis of the available information it can be pointed out that the number of post-graduate departments in social sciences in the universities and in the affiliated colleges nears a thousand; the number of students enrolled for the Master's degree in the various social sciences subjects is around 5,000 and the number of Ph D. students about 3,000. Percentage-wise, the total enrolment of students for the post-graduate work in social science disciplines is about 40 per cent of the total enrolment in the universities and colleges and the number of students registered for Ph D. is around 25 per cent of the total registrations.

In addition to the universities, there are about 1,000 institutions (including professional associations) engaged in research, teaching, training and counselling work in social sciences. These institutions are financed by the government and/or various private and public agencies.

As regards the social science manpower in the universities, it may be mentioned that the number of teachers of different categories in university departments and university colleges is around 3000 already. In addition to this number, there is substantial number of (more than 7,000) in the affiliated colleges. At the same time, technical institutions in various subjects such as engineering, medicine, agriculture, etc., have a substantial number of social scientists doing teaching and research work.

With this increase in the teaching and research activities in social science as well as in the manpower potential, the need for research journals has already been felt in different subject under social sciences and it is estimated that about 1,000 research journals are already being published in the country. In addition to the articles in these journals, a large quantity of research material is being published in India in the form of books, survey reports, seminars/conferences/workshops proceedings, etc.

In addition to the increase in the quantity of the documents in social sciences, a significant change has also taken place in the structure of the subjects in social sciences because of inter- disciplinary and multi-disciplinary research in these fields. This research in social sciences has received considerable support from the Planning Commission which set-up a Research Programmes Committee to fund plan-relevant research proposals submitted by research scholars. These research scholars get funds from various other organisations as well, like the Indian Council of Social Science Research, Indian Council of Historical Research, Indian Council of Philosophical Research and University Grants Commission, etc.

All these developments in the teaching and research activities in social sciences have made it essential that the information being generated through these activities is not only published properly but also stored and disseminated in the best possible manner so as to make this information resource really meaningful and productive. For this purpose a national information policy as well as network is much desired.

Facilities for Dissemination of Information in India

Historical Background

Parallel to the establishment and development of Indian National Scientific Documentation Centre (1952), there had been considerable interest among professional circles for the idea of establishing a similar centre in the social sciences. This idea gained further attention after the establishment of the Unesco Research Centre in Social Sciences in India.

For the first time, professional opinion was expressed at the national level on the occasion of the Library Seminar on Research in the Social Sciences held under the joint auspices of Indian School of International Studies and Indian Council of World Affairs in 1959. The Seminar recommended the establishment of Indian National Documentation Centre for Social Sciences for promoting documentation services in the country. This initiative was carried forward next year at Seminar on Bibliographical Organisation and Control in India held under the auspices of Indian Library Association in Calcutta in 1960. This Seminar laid stress on coordinating and supplementing the activities and programmes of various subject specialised centres by the proposed documentation centre. About 13 agencies were enumerated which were to take care of documentation in their respective fields of specialisation. It was, thus, for the first time that the idea of sectoral information system was mooted but only implicitly. The discussion of a plan for establishing a Social Science Documentation Centre almost became an annual affair, in the sense that the issue cropped up practically at every annual gathering of Librarians after 1960. IASLIC Seminar held at Lucknow in 1964 took up the matter afresh by requesting the Central Government to take appropriate steps for the establishment of a Documentation Centre for Social Science. It was also suggested that a survey of existing documentation services in India be conducted. While the Calcutta Seminar favoured decentralisation, the Lucknow Seminar preferred centralisation for all practical purposes. IASLIC Conference held in Trivandrum in 1965 did not favour centralisation. The Conference appointed a sub-committee for making recommendations (before March 31, 1966) to the Planning Commission for incorporation in the national Plan.

The whole question came up again for a complete review on the occasion of Seminar on Social Science Research and Library Development in India held in 1967 under the joint auspices of Indian School of International Studies and Indian Council of World Affairs. The Seminar considered very comprehensively the whole question and urged the establishment of a National Documentation Centre, with a provision that a number of other institutions were to be financially assisted under the national Plan. The Seminar was of the view that the establishment of Documentation Centre should be linked to a National Library of Social Sciences. The Seminar was thus a step forward to recognise the principles of viewing national resources and documentation services holistically.

The national debate, that went on for a long time, proved to be extremely useful and this finally led to the establishment of erstwhile ICSSR Documentation Unit – *later* Social Science Documentation Centre (SSDC) and *now* National Social Science Documentation Centre (NASSDOC) – by ICSSR in 1969. The establishment of

NASSDOC has been the most significant development in the information field. NASSDOC launched several programmes and is now firmly established, ICSSR Regional Centres (Appendix-VIII) in cooperation with several universities as a decentralised activity were also established. NASSDOC has indeed provided a good foundation of building up INISS.

Existing Facilities

At the initiative of some libraries and institutions, it has been possible to develop indexing and abstracting services of the current literature in the field of social sciences. Perhaps there is a need for a critical review now about the adequacies or otherwise of all these tools and services. That will help to improve the usefulness of these services to the social scientists, researchers, decision-makers and managers.

Many government and academic/research libraries are also bringing out their local documentation lists providing current awareness services primarily to their own clientele based on literature received by them individually.

Some of the important indexing and abstracting services are given in Appendix-III.

SYSTEM DESIGN

Structure

The INISS would be a multi-tier system. The main components are:

1. INISS Focal Point.
2. INISS Network of Information Centres and Services.

Focal Point

INISS Focal Point would be advised and guided by an Advisory Committee. Under this, there will be an Executive Committee for overseeing and implementing the programmes and recommendations of the Advisory Committee. It would also be responsible for day-to-day decisions within the framework of the approved scheme. There will also be a number of ad hoc working groups and expert groups.

These groups would be constituted by the Advisory Committee for carrying out special studies, surveys, preparation of reports, criteria, guidelines, standards, formats, etc.

A small secretariat would be required to be set-up to carry out the work of the INISS Focal Point and to give support to the work of various committees and groups. In addition to a Chief Executive, there will be need for Divisional Heads for dealing with programmes, planning and policy and systems as well as specialists to look after different aspects of the schemes.

The functions of the INISS Focal Point would include:

1. Formulating of a policy for INISS;
2. Formulating of plan of action;
3. Establishing mechanisms of implementing the policy and plans;
4. Allocating finances for various programmes;
5. Coordination of activities with national and international organisations;
6. Formulation of criteria, guidelines and standards;
7. Promoting and supporting research and development;
8. Promoting education and training programmes in information field and seeker user education;
9. Monitoring and evaluation of the performance of the system; and
10. Acting as a point of interaction with world information services, systems and programmes.

INISS Network

The INISS network would comprise:

1. National Centres of Information.
2. Regional Centres of Information.
3. Sectoral System.
4. Other Specialised Services.

As stated earlier, in developing the system, the main consideration would be to make the maximum use of existing information resources and facilities. Wherever necessary, the existing centres would be upgraded by augmenting the infrastructure. Gaps in provision of information services, if any, would be identified and efforts will be made to fill them up.

National Centres of Information

The national centres would be responsible for conducting, organising and providing information at national level in an overall manner in the field of social sciences. They have to be mission-oriented information centres and would take care of mostly residual services not covered by the sectoral system. The following centres would constitute the National Centres of Information in the field of social sciences.

1. National Social Science Documentation Centre (NASSDOC) *(Existing)* .
2. National Social Science Library (NASSLIB) *(Proposed)*.
3. National Social Science Data Archives (NASSDAR) (ICSSR Data Archives) *(Existing)*.

NASSDOC

NASSDOC has been in existence (first as erstwhile ICSSR Documentation unit and then Social Sciences Documentation Centre) since 1970. It is now firmly established. It has been undertaking several major projects either directly or in collaboration with some selected institutions. It has also promoted implementation of many projects under its grant-in-aid scheme. Under INISS scheme the activities of NASSDOC could be stepped up several fold. The following programmes are mentioned in this connection.

1. Bringing out current awareness service on Indian social science literature as an indexing or abstracting service;
2. Bringing out current awareness service on selected social science foreign literature in fields which cover many sectors or where no sectoral information centre exists;
3. Bringing out state-of-the-art reports on selected subjects;
4. Centralised acquisition of commercially available foreign machine-readable bibliographic data bases and offering SDI and retrospective search services;
5. Creating data bases for socio-economic information and or-

ganising dissemination service therefrom;

6. Establishing of on-going research information service;
7. Developing of access tools such as directories of periodicals, research institutions, societies, specialists, information sources and facilities, etc., in the field of social sciences;
8. Offering referral services and answering technical enquiries;
9. Undertaking literature search and compilation of bibliographies against specific requests and in anticipation;
10. Procuring copies of documents, on request, from whichever source available;
11. Providing translation service from foreign as well as Indian regional languages;
12. Providing reprographic facilities for copying documents and distributing information;
13. Undertaking periodical surveys for assessing information needs and uses in the country;
14. Organising programmes for creation of information consciousness among users;
15. Organising user training programmes;
16. Organising training facilities in information science with special emphasis on social sciences;
17. Carrying out and supporting research in social science information;
18. Providing advisory services to other information centres in social sciences; and
19. Developing relations and cooperation with national and international organisations engaged in social science information.

NASSLIB

The development of NASSLIB is closely linked to the programme and activities of NASSDOC. It will be developed initially within NASSDOC as an institutional project and later on made a separate institution. NASSLIB will be based on the cooperative acquisition concept. It will not duplicate material already available in India. It will endeavour to supplement the national collection by way of filling up gaps. It will survey the information resources already available in and identify gaps in order to assume responsibility for filling them up.

This concept would mean that as far as possible the materials will be located in actual places of use and this material should be bibliographically controlled through Union Catalogue to make it available to any user wherever he may be. The ultimate aim would be that NASSLIB and the other service libraries in social sciences will together ensure that at least one copy of everything worthwhile, being published throughout the world in the field of social science, will be available within the country, no matter where it will be kept, for use by scholars at all times to come. The main responsibility of NASSLIB, among others, would be:

1. To build a comprehensive world collection of social science material by way of supplementing the national collections;
2. To maintain a good collection of reference publications in the field of social sciences to enable carrying out of the bibliographical tasks;
3. To maintain a comprehensive collection of Indian material in social sciences including theses, government publications, reports, etc;
4. To offer consultation, reference and inter-library loan service as well as reprography services;
5. To maintain up-to-date national union catalogue of social science material in machine-readable form for promoting use of material as well as for following cooperative acquisition policy; and
6. To maintain dormitories for storing older research material weeded out by service libraries.

NASSDAR

ICSSR Data Archives, set-up in 1973, initiated inventorising quantitative data, and processing it into organised collection to promote and augment research. It is currently engaged in compiling inventory of data generating by various Research Institutions in India since 1951. Guidance and consultancy services to scholars relating to their problems of data processing through computer, are also provided by the ICSSR Data Archives. And as such, under INISS scheme, ICSSR Data Archives may be designated National Social Science Data Archives (NASSDAR). Broad objectives of NASSDAR would, among others, include:

1. Promoting and coordinating organisation of data relevant for

research in easy processable form;
2. Helping research scholars to have access to data gathered by various governmental agencies as also other research institutions, and to liaison between data gathering agencies and data users, and
3. Developing skills and competence among researchers in computer application in social science research and in secondary analysis of data.

For realisation of these objectives, the functions of NASSDAR would be:

(i) To build up
- (a) Data Repository;
- (b) Institution-based Data Bank
- (c) Clearing House

(ii) To create
- (a) Data base for National Register of Social Scientists
- (b) Inventory of Governmental and Non-Governmental Organisations engaged in social science research and thereby in creation of data.

(iii) To provide
- (a) Guidance and consultancy in Data processing
- (b) Training in computer application
- (c) Grant-in-Aid for Data organisation.

Regional System

ICSSR has already established Regional Centres at Bombay, Calcutta, Chandigarh, Hyderabad, New Delhi and Shillong (Appendix-VIII). These Regional Centres are assigned the responsibility of building basic reference collection in social sciences not already available at the Universities/Institutions with which these centres are associated.

Under the new programme envisaged for the future, the role and functions of the Regional Centres will have to be modified considerably. The present Regional Centres are located in cities which have a heavy concentration of research libraries in social sciences and are well stocked with scholarly material. They are also attached to established Universities/Institutions. These Regional Centres also cover the various regions of the country adequately. They should be made use of essentially for utilising the literature resources available in the country for the benefit of the entire scholarly community. The main objectives of the Regional Centres would be:

1. To survey the information resources of the region and to organise their mobilisation for meeting the information demands of the region;
2. To establish, maintain, update and publish regional union catalogue of literature resources;
3. To establish a strong reprographic unit and to serve the region with reprographic copies of information sources;
4. To procure, on request, documents within and outside the region;
5. To build and maintain a good collection of reference material for the benefit of scholars;
6. To collect and build a good collection of social science literature in the regional languages; and
7. To provide a referral service to the seekers/users in the region.

Thus the Regional Centres would be set-up, funded and administrated directly under the INISS scheme. They will have separate physical facilities of their own, though housed in a university campus. They will be equipped with a good range of reprography equipment. They will be provided with vehicles for the purpose of inter-library borrowings. In vast country like India, where the literature resources are widely scattered, the Regional Centres will be of help in mobilising the resources for the benefit of the entire scholarly community. In this manner, the development of information resources can be decentralised. While the collections, as far as possible, will be kept in actual places of use, they will be at the same time made accessible to any seeker/user in the country, through the document supply service of the Regional Centres.

Sectoral Information System

The sectoral system is the vital link in INISS. Sectoral Centres are discipline-oriented or mission-oriented. They would be developed from the most suitable research institutions in the discipline/mission concerned, which has already developed a strong information base. The facilities of the local unit would be augmented and it would be upgraded to provide service on a national scale. These Sectoral Centres would provide specialised services with a good amount of subject competence. They will be manned mostly by subject specialists trained in information work. Their services are expected to play an essential role in the flow of information by maintaining close touch with current research and practice and by keeping in close association with the seekers/users. They would select, evaluate and synthesise information in well-defined special fields, and/or in areas pertinent to scientific disciplines/missions and present it in a form best suited to the needs of seekers/users.

The sectoral system would consist of the leading centres chosen for the purpose as well as all other information centres, belonging to discipline/mission. They will together form a grid of their own and will take care of development of information resources as well as services in a holistic manner. The Sectoral Information System would provide the following services:

(i) Specialised current indexing and abstracting services including SDI;
(ii) Subject bibliographies;
(iii) Subject union catalogues;
(iv) Information retrieval;
(v) Collection and dissemination of technical and socio-economic information;
(vi) Translation and document supply; and
(vii) Preparation of surveys, state-of-the-art reports, forecasting reports, techno-economic and management information.

In addition, the Sectoral Centres would build up and maintain a document collection supplementing those of the institutions in the sector. They would coordinate the information services within the sector. They may offer advisory service and assistance to the local information units. They would build up data banks relevant to their scope and activity. They would envisage developing computer based information services for the sector in cooperation with national information centres and ensuring national and international compatibility. They would develop relations and maintain cooperation with foreign information centres, research institutions, professional bodies, etc., for evolving exchange of information.

The Sectoral Centres would be developed in major areas of national relevance and priority. At least ten centres could be developed during the Eighth Plan period. They will contribute a great deal towards building up the information infrastructure in the country in the fields of social sciences.

Local Information Units

As mentioned earlier, the lowest level of information centres, called Local Information Units, would operate in research institutions, academic institutions, government agencies, industrial enterprises, etc. They are expected to offer personalised services to seekers/users in their parent institutions. They belong to the sectoral system relating to their area of specialisation. They would be responsible for feeding information generated by their institutions to the sectoral centres.

THRUST AND ACTIVITIES

The ultimate aim of INISS is to develop the national information infrastructure in so far as social sciences are concerned, for supporting research and scholarly pursuits. Towards this aim, certain major activities and services have to be given a thrust.

Needs and Uses

Survey of information needs and uses as well as the resources available would have to be undertaken at national, regional, sectoral and institutional levels so that the functioning of the different tiers of INISS network could be planned in relation to actual needs and uses and that adequate resources and facilities could be built up for meeting them.

Resources Development

A policy for coordinating the acquisition of documents and their distribution among different libraries would be followed in order that:

1. libraries do not have an unnecessary stock,

2. there is no undue duplication of material among libraries, and
3. available book purchase fund of the country is made optimum use of for acquiring maximum number of titles. The acquisition policies and profiles of each institution would be clearly defined and coordinated within the sector, region and at national level. The coordination may include mutually agreed upon acquisition profiles of institutions and subscription to periodicals and serials.

In the matter of information resources development, a programme of decentralisation has to be followed. Most important material would be available in the institutional libraries, that is, in the actual place of use. The Sectoral Centre would supplement the acquisition of individual institutions coming under its purview so as to ensure availability of an exhaustive collection in the area of the sector. The Regional Centre would—

(i) maintain a general reference library,
(ii) collect and hold theses and dissertations prepared in the region,
(iii) maintain a depository of publications of regional languages, and
(iv) act as a dormitory for housing older research material weeded out by service libraries. NASSLIB would build up a national collection by complementing the local, sectoral and regional collections. There are many residual areas to be taken care of by NASSLIB.

In the matter of building up the national collection, the goal would be that NASSLIB Regional Centres, Sectoral Centres and Local Units of individual libraries taken together would ensure that at least one accessible copy no matter where it is kept, is made available within the country for use by scholars at all times.

Union Catalogues

Setting up a decentralised network of collection building means that (1) the constituent libraries must use common techniques for processing the collections, and that (2) there should be a union catalogue for the purpose of interconnection and for readily locating the documents in the libraries. Besides serving as a location tool, union catalogues help in revealing strong and weak areas in the national collection for the purpose of continuing the acquisition programme.

NASSDOC has already taken up the union catalogue work and achieved good progress. This programme, which remaines suspended, has to be stepped up.

Some other individual efforts have also been made, e.g., CICIL series includes union catalogue of *Communication, Informatics and Librarianship* publication in Delhi.

Efforts would be made to store the information in machine-readable form and establish a mechanism for constant updating. In addition to the total national union catalogue, compilation of regional union catalogues and subject union catalogues would be attempted.

Data Banks

NASSDAR, NASSDOC and the Sectoral Centres would build up data/information bank relevant to their activities. The data bank has to cover R&D activities, completed and ongoing projects, status of R&D abroad and country profiles, management information, manpower, techno-economic information, statistical data, etc. The Sectoral Centres would set-up discipline-oriented data banks. They will select useful information, analyse it with user interests and store it in conventional or machine-readable form.

Current Awareness Services (CAS)

National Literature

NASSDOC should attempt to bring out *Indian Social Science Abstracts* to provide not only bibliographical control of domestic output but also to act as a feeder for coverage of Indian literature by major international abstracting and indexing services.

The Sectoral Centres would take care of the bibliographical control of unpublished literature.

Foreign Literature

Though in all major disciplines and branches of knowledge, international abstracting and indexing services are available, it would be desirable to prepare selective current awareness services with focus on the progress of work in India. It would be the responsibility of Sectoral Centres to offer such selective current awareness services.

Selective Dissemination of Information (SDI)

Indexing and abstracting services are now increasingly available in computer-prepared magnetic tapes. There are several such services available in social science fields also. But as they are costly, the acquisition of such tape services have to be initially centralised at NASSDOC, which in turn would generate and offer services for SDI as well as for retrospective search. It may be possible for Sectoral Centres to obtain group profiles relating to the field of interest and, in turn select, evaluate and synthesise information for transferring it to the seekers/users. The SDI service provides information which, as closely as possible, meets the interest profile of the seekers/user. Sectoral Centres can supply widely scattered seekers/users with the new knowledge they need to keep abreast with. They also constitute a means of making information-conscious potential seekers/users, who had been unaware of its importance. SDI services are offered better using a computer for which expertise in software and hardware capabilities exists in India.

Information Analysis/State-of-the-Art Reports/Surveys/Forecasts

Seekers/users today require carefully selected data and digested information which could be straightaway applied and assimilated. Information has to be (1) analysed, synthesised and evaluated, keeping in view the interests of the seekers users, and (2) to be served promptly. The seekers/users may not be satisfied with raw data and mere bibliographic citations. They may want the actual information for direct application. For this purpose, the source documents have to be analysed, pertinent information culled out, evaluated and served. This type of work is normally known as Information Analysis and the Sectoral Centres are expected to offer this service. Reviews, State-of-the-Art Reports, Surveys, Forecasts, etc., are products of information analysis.

Referral Service

Those who are in need of information should be able to know which source should give them the precise information and whom to consult for the purpose. A referral service, as regards who is doing what, where to get what, etc., should be set-up to direct the inquirers to the sources of information for the purpose of establishing contact directly. The referral service should be organised at the National and Sectoral levels.

Promoting Use of Information

Information ought to have its market so as to derive its fullest benefits. There is a need to create and step up demand for information. Ways and means have to be found to make potential seekers/users information-conscious. Programmes like organising group discussions, demonstrations, seminars, etc., will have to be taken up.

Proper facilities for training in the use of information have to be organised. The training will help to improve the seekers'/users' attitude to information and would promote use of information.

Manpower Development

Proper training facilities, specially oriented to social science information, should be organised in order to take care of the manpower requirement for developing INISS. This would be by way of supplementing the existing facilities with particular emphasis to social sciences. Regular courses, short-term courses, refresher courses, in-service training, etc., should be available for meeting various requirements.

Provision should also be made for carrying out research in social science information. Organising symposia, seminars, workshops, etc., to enable the information scientists to share and exchange their experiences should also be taken care of by INISS.

Budget and Strategy

The total outlay (capital and recurring) for development of INISS over a period of five years is estimated at Rs. 708 lakhs (Table 9.1).

This includes provision for—

(1) INISS Secretariat,
(2) Strengthening of NASSDOC,
(3) Establishment of NASSLIB,
(4) Strengthening of NASSDAR,
(5) Setting up of six Regional Centres and eight Sectoral Centres, and
(6) Carrying out some centralised services.

TABLE 9.1: Broad Indication of the Financial Outlay of INISS

(in lakhs of Rs.)

	I Year	II Year	III Year	IV Year	V Year	Total
National Focal Point Secretariat	1.000	1.500	2.000	2.500	3.000	10.000
National Centres						
NASSDOC	25.000	28.000	30.000	32.000	35.000	150.000
NASSLIB	20.000	20.000	15.000	10.000	10.000	75.000
NASSDAR	25.000	28.000	30.000	32.000	35.000	150.000
Regional Centres						
6 Centres (2 in Year I 2 in Year II 2 in Year III)	8.000	16.000	22.000	18.000	14.000	78.000
Sectoral Centres						
8 Centres (3 in Year I 2 in Year II 2 in Year III 1 in Year IV)	15.000	40.000	45.000	50.000	45.000	195.000
Centralised Services	5.000	8.000	10.000	12.000	15.000	50.00
Total	99.000	151.500	154.00	156.500	157.000	708.000

The estimates have been based on the analogy of the National Information System for Science and Technology, but on reduced scale for development of INISS. For example, the Non-Plan budget of INSDOC is now over Rs. 50 lakhs and only half of this input is proposed for stepping up the activities of NASSDOC. The National Science Library is planned at an estimated cost of Rs. 125 lakhs whereas an investment of Rs. 75 lakhs is proposed for NASSLIB. Under the NIS-

SAT scheme, each Regional Centre would be provided with about Rs. 25 lakhs in a period of five years. In the INISS scheme, about half of the amount is proposed for developing the Regional Centres. Similar is also the case with the Sectoral Centres. If we compare the existing level of investment in the NISSAT, it would be seen that the proposed investment for INISS is not only realistic but also modest.

Summary

The Ministry of Human Resource Development, through ICSSR-NASSDOC, should be responsible for the INISS scheme. The ICSSR-NASSDOC should be vested with appropriate powers to coordinate the information activities in social sciences. It should also be provided with adequate funds. The nucleus of developing INISS would be the existing resources and facilities available in a number of organisations and institutions, universities, government departments, etc. The functioning of the system would be at several levels, viz., National Centres, Regional Centres, Sectoral Centres and Local Information Units. Active participation of all the constituent institutions is a *sine-qua-non* for achieving an integrated Indian National Information System for Social Sciences. This national system will enable research workers, scholars, academicians, management personnel, etc., to have access to information economically, efficiently and expeditiously.

BACKGROUNDERS

Abha Kumar, 1979, *National Information System : Literature Survey: MLIS Dissertation,* Vikram University, Ujjain

Agrawal, S.P., 1984, Horizons in National Information System in Social Science, *Indian Book Industry* 29(5), January-February, p 86-95.

Agrawal, S.P. and Manohar Lal, 1984, National Information Policy: Evolution and Future Direction, *Library Herald* 23(2-3), p 90-98.

Anon, 1974, *UNESCO Information Policy Objectives: UNISIST Proposals,* UNESCO, Paris, 26p., SC/74/WS/3

Anon, 1976, *National Information Policy: National Information Systems (NATIS)*, UNESCO, Paris, 26p., CON 76/NATIS/60.

Anon, 1986, *National Information Policy on Library and Information System : A Presentation,* Committee on National Policy on Library and Information System, New Delhi, 30p.

Anon, 1987, *Background to Evolving a National Information Policy,* 2nd edn., Lok Sabha Secretariat, New Delhi, v, 39p.

Deenadayalu, C., 1986, National Policy on Library and Information System, *Rilisar Bulletin* 4(1), p 44-45.

Eswara Reddy, D.B., 1984, National Library Policy for Higher Education and Research in India, *Lucknow Librarian* 16(2), p 45-52.

Goil, N.K., 1984, National Information System, *Library Herald* 16(1-2) April-September, p 73-77.

Gupta, B.M. and Jain, V.K., eds., 1990, *Handbook of Libraries, Archives and Information Centres in India*, Vol. 8, *Social Sciences Information Systems and Centres*, Aditya Prakashan, Delhi, 276p.

Iyengar, T.K.S., 1988, The Information Community: Vital Link for Progress in Third World Countries, *University News* 26(37) September 12, p 5-7.

Johry, K.K., 1985, Towards National Information Policy, *Hindu* (Newspaper) July 30, p 17, col 1.

Judge, P.J., 1971, Policy Issues and the Development of Information Systems, *Aslib Proceedings* 23(7) July, p 351-361.

Kamath, V.A., 1978, Role of Information Systems in National Development, *Commerce*, Annual Number, p 185-192.

Kumar, P.S.G., 1985, Information Service for National Development. The Indian Context, *Herald of Library Science* 24(1-2) p 30-35.

Neelameghan, A., 1979, Regional Development Information Systems: Their Role in Developing Regions, *Library Science with a Slant to Documentation* 16(3) September, p 91-98.

Parthasarathi, Ashok, 1988, Informatics for Development: The Indian Experience, *Mainstream* 26(41) July 23, p 26-30.

Rajagopalan, T.S. and Rajan, T.N., 1983, Vital Components of Information Systems: Institutions and Human Resources, *Library Science with a Slant to Documentation* 20(4), p 191-204.

Soni, P., 1988, Impact of Informatics on Future Social Change, *Management and Labour Studies* 13(1) p. 59-65.

10

INDIAN NATIONAL INTER-LIBRARY RESOURCES CENTRE FOR SOCIAL SCIENCES (INILRCES)

(Proposed)

Introduction

Although the tradition of teaching and research in social sciences in India is of recent origin, the concern over the outcome of rapid changes and the response of the Indian academic community to developments abroad have contributed to the speedy growth of social sciences in the country. In the face of ever-burgeoning materials, published and otherwise, it is almost impossible for a single library to cope with all the needs of its users.

To keep pace with the information explosion, various methods have been suggested or practised the world over. These include structured pattern of libraries leading to the development of repositories and resource sharing. In India, we had embarked on a new experiment — the Inter-Library Resources Centre — to collect reading matter and research tools for scholars, combining the salient features of inter-library lending and a repository for resource sharing in the process.

Resource Sharing

Resource sharing is a term with wider connotations than cooperation. It is an essential element in providing library and information services, sufficient to meet the needs of a country's economic and social development.

The objectives of "resource sharing" can be achieved through various organisational arrangements called the consortium, the network or the cooperative. Generally, the term "resource" signifies a thing, a person or action, which is handy in times of need. "Resource sharing" involves reciprocity; it is "a partnership in which each member has something useful to contribute to others and which each is willing to make available when needed. Resource sharing denotes a mode of operation whereby functions are shared in common by a number of libraries".

The justification of resource sharing, particularly in India, is apparent from the fact that libraries organising research collections have to spend a lion's share of their acquisition budgets in purchasing materials that are seldom, if ever, used. The libraries, in this context, should strive more and more to realise "use" as well as "non-use" in terms of the acquisition budgets earmarked for each category. And this brings them logically to the resource sharing efforts.

Inter-Library Lending

A traditional and tested method to this end is the "Inter-Library Lending System", but it has certain limitations. When the number of these transactions is small and not a daily occurrence, the inter-library loan system is both cheap and quick. But if the transactions are more frequent, they tend to be more complex and also costlier. Different libraries have different rules on loaning their materials. Some, for example, do not send out periodicals as a matter of rule, while some others stipulate that the loaned material must be used in the premises of the borrowing library. The security and care of the loan-material poses delicate issues, which are sometimes insoluble.

Repositories

The "repository" concept is generally equated with "the storage, preservation and continued availability of low-use material discarded by libraries through lack of space". Few libraries play the role of a repository exclusively, many of them continue, in themselves, the functions of a repository as well as the "usual" library.

Repositories are precluded from taking an active part in national inter-lending or acquisition systems because of lack of ability or willingness to transfer library stock, paucity of suitable building and shortage of trained manpower, and also because of "user perceptions of their need for on-site access".

In the absence of clear-cut legislative guidelines there are sharp differences of opinion on what stock should be relegated to a repository, and the decisions have to be left to the discretionary whims of the relegating library, which is frequently weak in methods of transfer and in maintaining the catalogue and other records.

Repositories, it has been emphasised, are not glamorous. "They do not have the immediacy of on-line retrieval, the excitement of new techniques, even the human satisfaction of community information services. And yet, they are fundamental to all library and information activities, and it is shortsighted to concentrate on the techniques of information exploitation if the information itself is being slowly but inexorably lost".

Resources Centre

Another method, which is of far-reaching significance in terms of sharing resources among several libraries, is to establish a Centre, where different libraries could deposit such research material as are not used frequently by them, and the Centre, in its turn, would be responsible for organising the materials and making them available to all visiting scholars. Obviously, this alternative would be a great service to research workers. If the service is properly organised, researchers will not be required to visit different libraries in search of material now concentrated at the Centre in a substantially large quantity.

A Centre of this kind has several added advantages, which include:

(i) Depositing libraries could have increased space on their shelves after their less used volumes are removed to the Centre. They can fill the vacuum with more recent books needed by their regular users;

(ii) Authorities of the depositing libraries could also have the satisfaction that the research material acquired by them painstakingly over several years could now be used profitably and more frequently by a large number of local as well as out-station social scientists;

(iii) Care and preservation of their materials ensured, the depositing libraries could have their budget allocations used for other purposes;

(iv) Any lacunae in the collections from anyone particular depositing library could be filled up by the materials deposited by other libraries at the Centre. This is particularly true to the gaps in the back files of periodicals which are very expensive to fill; and

(v) A spirit of active and meaningful cooperation would be generated among the libraries, which could vie with one another to extend their cooperation to other spheres, and all this could lead to a better service to their users. These libraries could, in the circumstances, share acquisition programmes to step up specialisation, cataloguing and programming to secure consistency and uniformity as also micro-filming programmes.

The Centre may also undertake to establish and maintain a Union Catalogue of foreign monographs currently acquired by all or selected depositing libraries if each of them could send a card to the Centre for every new foreign monograph acquired by them. A Union Catalogue of this type along with the Union Catalogue of Social Sciences Serials would be yet another information tool on the growing resources for social science research in the libraries.

The establishment of the Centre can help evolve a well-coordinated system, under which the unit libraries may overcome local difficulties of staff, space and budget.

Delhi Scene

The capital city of Delhi has perhaps the largest cluster of libraries which may be broadly divided into four groups:

(i) Academic libraries which include the libraries of the universities and colleges. These are naturally multifocal in their acquisition, i.e., they have acquired and preserved, over many years, printed materials in the form of books, periodicals and pamphlets in various disciplines of knowledge including social sciences for the needs of their students and faculties;

(ii) Government of India libraries which are more restricted in their scope. Each of them has acquired and preserved, for several years. Printed materials in the form of books, periodicals, pamphlets and also government publications primarily on such subjects as are within the scope of activities of its parent body, which may be either the Ministry, its department or attached or subordinate office. Since the total governmental activities are comprehensive of all phases of social life, almost all Government of India libraries are resource bases for social research;

(iii) Libraries of autonomous institutions which are even more specialised than Government of India libraries. Each of these institutions has very specific activities and most the institutions are devoted to study and research in particular branches of social sciences, e.g., the Indian Institution of Public Administration, Institute of Defence Studies and Analysis, Institute of Foreign Trade, Institute of Applied Manpower Research, Indian Law Institute, and so on.

(iv) Public libraries which are established to cater to the needs of general public. Public libraries also often develop special collections, e.g., Delhi Public Library, Delhi.

The total number of libraries of all these categories in Delhi would be around 150. Many of these libraries were established long before Independence, although quite a few have come into existence only after 1947. As reservoirs of research material, about half of these libraries are known to have large collections of social science material. A rough estimate is that they would have, between them, over 20 lakh volumes and their total annual intake by purchase, gift and exchange would exceed 100,000 titles. There are over 1000 library trained personnel engaged in these libraries, and annual maintenance cost including staff salary, book budgets and other services would be over Rs. 5 crores. Delhi thus has a vast resource base for research in social sciences and it is expanding year after year by the establishment of new institutions and by additional funds becoming available.

An inevitable feature of such a situation is that (i) a good deal of resource materials has become duplicated, (ii) some of it is available at only a few places, and (iii) some needed material is perhaps nowhere available among the libraries in the city. None of these libraries has become, or will ever become, self-sufficient for its actual or potential needs. Moreover, most of these libraries have grown and are growing beyond their available space capacity. In consequence, the material which is ordinarily less frequently used gets crowded on shelves in two or three rows and also gets relatively less attended to, as far as its maintenance is concerned. As a result, even the material which was once known to be available is not often located quickly for subsequent use. Yet another disadvantage to the researcher in social sciences is that he has to go from one library to another in search of the material (and only) in anticipation that the required material may become available on time in pursuit of several libraries. In this, the researcher faces some odd situations. Many of the government libraries require special passes to visit them. There are not always good reading facilities provided in some libraries. Most libraries function during normal office hours only and the paucity of staff and space in many of these libraries renders the use of the material somewhat difficult for a research worker visiting Delhi for a short period.

Indian Council of Social Science Research (ICSSR) with its primary objective since its perception in 1969 to promote research in social sciences took note of this situation and initiated several programmes, some time-bound and some continuing, but all aimed at facilitating social science research. One such important programme has been the compilation of Union Catalogue of Social Science Periodicals and Serials. The Union Catalogue enables a person to locate Social Sciences Serials and Periodicals available in important libraries of India. On the completion of the first phase of Union Catalogue project, the compilation of a Retrospective Index of Indian Social Science Periodicals was taken up followed by "Area Studies Bibliographies" and "Languages Bibliographies".

Inter-Library Resources Centre

In 1973, the Jawaharlal Nehru University (JNU) jointly with ICSSR established Inter-Library Resources Centre (ILRC). For this purpose, JNU made available the library wing of its building at 35, Ferozeshah Road, New Delhi, and the facilities of the hostel nearby. The main office of ILRC at Ferozeshah Road is very centrally located as far as the libraries having a large collection of social science research material are concerned and is open for use by the general public. To begin with, ICSSR invited a meeting of the librarians of the important libraries in Delhi and requested them to deposit only such of their back files of Social Science Periodicals which were not too often in use in their libraries.

The response was very good. ICSSR, therefore, made formal arrangements to accept the deposits of back files of Social Science Periodicals, Newspapers and Government Documents. Under this scheme a dozen local libraries, to begin with, deposited with ILRC materials — non-current and infrequently used yet important from the point of research. The idea caught on and the number of participating libraries including National Social Science Documentation Centre of ICSSR rose to 38. The deposits were accepted on condition that the proprietary right of each depositing library in respect of its national would be respected and the material would be preserved and made available for consultation on the premises. The depositing libraries could withdraw their deposits temporarily or permanently if they so desired. They could also gift the material to ILRC at their will. Several libraries gifted some of the material. The material was processed in a simple manner to enable its quick location for use. The depository collection attracts visitors wishing to use this material because the back files of journals, research reports and government documents are now available for consultation under one roof.

Service

In setting up ILRC, the objective has been not simply of accumulating Social Science research material at one place, but to provide a variety of services to the community of researchers, including among others, the following:

(i) To the researchers who are stationed in Delhi, ILRC is within easy reach. ILRC remained, at one time, open on all days of the year except January 26, August 15, and October 2, from 8.30 to 7.30 p.m. It was initially planned that in course of time the working hours of ILRC would be extended to facilitate its use for longer hours on working days as well as Sundays and other holidays. This, however, could not be worked out because of bureaucratic hampers;

(ii) For persons stationed elsewhere in India, a scheme of Study Grants provided for two-way travel and a modest allowance per day for lodging and boarding. Efforts are made to provide accommodation in the JNU hostel nearby.

(iii) ILRC provides reprographic service so that readable photocopies of required articles from periodicals or of reasonable extracts from other documents in the Centre are supplied on a cost basis to local as well as outside scholars.

The charges at present are Rs. 0.60 per exposure.

(iv) ILRC also provides short bibliographies on specific subjects on demand, tailored to the needs of the research scholar, on a nominal charge; and

(v) For inter-library loan services, the Centre also maintains a carrier service so that the periodical volumes or documents which are not available in the Centre but are available in some other library in Delhi can be obtained on loan for consultation in its premises. The 32 volumes of *Union Catalogue of Social Science Periodicals and Serials*, which have already been published, enable to find out the location of periodicals volumes in any of the libraries in Delhi.

It was, at one time, rightly proposed to connect ILRC at New Delhi with ICSSR Regional Centres set-up outside Delhi. Unfortunately, however, it did not work out.

Constraints

Normally monetary and man-power resources create bottlenecks. But in the case of ILRC it is not so, if past experience, achievements and performance of ILRC are any indication.

The role of resource sharing in collecting available information materials — old and current — from various sources systematically, organising, preserving and making them available to the seekers users speedily has been recognised. What probably is not appreciated is that no resource sharing network can perform this role if efforts lack sincerity of purpose.

I have always felt and said that unfortunately, an awareness of the requirements of resource sharing and networking as a base of the effective library services in the context of national planning and development is generally lacking in our country. Resource sharing concept has so far received only lip sympathy of those who matter and administrators are generally too preoccupied to pay heed to what resource sharing concept entails. Even intellectuals and known-to-be-library-lovers when they happen to be at the decision-making level tend to neglect, rather act to dismantle whatsoever structure is there, just for the sake of administrative convenience and immediate short-term benefits; and this despite sufficient realisation that decision-making should be done on the basis of proven results. Such patrons whom the library set-up and resource sharing network had served so well in their research pursuits, do not show the slightest hesitation in doing this disservice and that too giving the library set-up no chance to point out the likely negative results of such hasty unilateral action Libraries and networking today are in fact laboratories for experimentations for such academics.

There is also the danger within inasmuch as we professionals help or hate the resource-sharing concept according to our own personal vested interests and future prospects, because of our ambitions rather than the institutional interest.

The attitude of starting a profit-sharing centre, and not resource-sharing centre also seems to have crept in. These disastrous attitudes are serious constraints which need to be debated. It would, therefore, not be out of place to draw the attention of all concerned — administrators, intellectuals, professionals and social scientists — to their obligations towards strengthening of the concept of a centre of inter-library resources as also towards continued development and growth of the centre to enable it to provide the services vis-a-vis the needs of the research community and the economy of country.

Looking back, the ILRC set-up so painstakingly built up, stands dismantled at present — the number of participating libraries dwindling to 28 sleeping partners (Appendix-IX) — not because of any weakness of its own, but because of the faulty vision of those in position.

11

INDIAN NATIONAL DOCUMENT SUPPLY SYSTEM IN SOCIAL SCIENCES (INDOCSIS)

(Proposed)

Introduction

The foremost objective of libraries is to provide documents demanded by seekers/scholars. In the present conditions it is not an easy task to cope with. This is because, on the one hand, there is a phenomenal increase in published and unpublished material, and on the other, increasing publishing costs have rendered libraries less and less self-sufficient. Developments in bibliographic sources are reflected in increased demand for access to documents. With all the efforts going into indexing, storage and retrieval of references, it will be utterly frustrating for both professionals and the seekers/users if the documents referred to cannot be obtained. Non-availability of a document, however, does not always mean that it is not physically available in a particular library or libraries but that it is not located on demand. We have, therefore, to devise ways and means to increase access to records and materials to two groups of people : (1) librarians, and (2) seekers/users. Dr. S.R. Ranganathan emphasised this aspect of service when he said, "Every reader his book". It is, therefore, imperative that the information system as a whole should have a mechanism to ensure supply of a required document or a copy of it to the seeker/user. "Universal Availability of Publications (UAP)" is now considered a necessary concomitant to "Universal Bibliographical Control of Publications". The aim of UAP is to provide a document in original or its copy in any form to the intending seeker/user in any part of the world.

Scope

A plan of document supply service in the Capital city of Delhi, where a large cluster of libraries of different types exists, is appended. The experiment can also be followed in other metropolitan cities leading to a network of document supply centres in India. Social sciences here include disciplines corresponding to the definition given by the *Encyclopaedia Britannica*, that social sciences "concern the disciplines that deal with human behaviour in its social and cultural aspects — Economics, Political Science, Sociology, Social and Cultural Anthropology, Social Psychology and Social and Economic geography".

Organisational Models

The document supply service can be organised according to anyone or the combination of the following models:

(i) Centralised at a single institution with partial dependence on a small number of individual libraries;
(ii) Decentralised and spread over a large number of libraries but planned and coordinated and linked by location tools like Union Catalogues so as to achieve maximum coverage of source documents; and
(iii) Decentralised on several libraries without any access tool to each others' holdings.

All these models have been tried with varying degrees of success in different countries. Activities of a few organisations is mentioned below.

United Kingdom (U.K.)

In U.K., British Library Lending Division (BLLD) is an example of the first model. It has extensive acquisition programme which includes all significant periodicals regardless of language, all important worthwhile English language monographs and all available report literature. It supplements its own stock with a Union Catalogue of other libraries holdings and by cooperation with regional interlending organisations in U.K.

United States of America (USA)

In USA (different to centralised practice in the U.K.) 300 networks, consortia and other cooperative library organisations, without any pre-planned central coordination, are engaged in document supply activity as their primary function. Some of the networks linked with Union Catalogue activity and supported by latest information technology, like Ohio College Library Centre (OCLC) Automated System, have facilitated interlending at reduced cost and greater speed of service. West Central Illinois Library Cooperative System works without centralised locational tool but is linked by a highly structured tele-type transmission loop for the routing of request through central processing point in the Western Illinois University to the member libraries. An average of four to five days are taken in the delivery of a document. SUNY/OCLC (State University of New York/OCLC) is another network which provides fast and efficient State-wise delivery of inter-library loan material by using OCLC Inter-Loan Sub-System.

Russia (Erstwhile)

In the USSR, Lenin State Library (erstwhile) provides document supply service at national level. It also supplies copies of Soviet publications requested by other countries. Its stock includes Soviet publications collected under Legal Deposit Law and supported by periodical holdings catalogue. Since 1955, over 500 libraries have been contributing to the catalogue.

Germany

Like the USA, document supply structure in Germany (erstwhile Federal Republic of Germany) is decentralised but coordinated as a cooperative programme by the Deutsche Forschungs Gemeinschaft which also provides financial assistance to the members to strengthen their stock. The system is based on identifying libraries specialising in specific subject disciplines such as Law, Medicine, Psychology, or particular form of publications like periodicals, official publications, newspapers, etc. Location tools available are seven Regional Union Catalogues supplemented by Central Subject Catalogue (available also in microform), Berlin Periodicals Data Base and other Union Catalogue Projects.

India

In India, document supply is greatly confined to inter-library loan and supply of a photocopy of the desired document. The activity is taken up on an individual library level. There has so far been no organisational set-up at national or sub-national level to take up document supply as its primary activity, though location tools have been compiled in specific disciplines by various universities and documentation centres. In certain cities, sporadic efforts have been made to develop resource sharing activities to meet demands. Indian National Scientific Documentation Centre (INSDOC) and National Social Science Documentation Centre (NASSDOC) have taken up document supply service within their specialised disciplines at national level. INSDOC has been developing National Science Library to support the service. NASSDOC, to support document supply in periodical literature, set-up Inter-Library Resources Centre (ILRC) in collaboration with Jawaharlal Nehru University, to accept as deposit/gratis from libraries in Delhi, serial material which is infrequently used but is important for research, i.e., Government reports, journals, newspapers, etc. Regretfully it is almost suspended at present. The document supply system in Delhi generally works on "gentlemen's understanding" and few libraries refuse to lend a document unless it is restricted for certain reasons.

In India, organisational structure could be decentralised as in the USA and coordinated at national level forming part of national information network. The National Committee on Regional Library Cooperation in the U.K. suggested, in its report on the future pattern of interlending that, the best pattern was for each to build on its special strengths and thus together provide a comprehensive service to the country. But for certain categories of material (e.g., serials, report literature, conference proceedings and official publications) concentration at national level is required to avoid wasteful and ineffective duplication.

The above suggested model is feasible for structuring the Indian National Document Supply System in Social Sciences (INDOCSIS) in Delhi. Interlending nodes could be identified in Delhi on the basis of subject specialisation and/or form of literature held by them.

Library Scene in Delhi

There are about 100 social science libraries in Delhi, attached to government departments, research institutes, universities, commercial enterprises, etc. Some illustrative examples with respective subject specialisation are :

Economics	–	Rattan Tata Library, National Council of Applied Economic Research, Indian Institute of Foreign Trade;
Education	–	National Council of Educational Research and Training National Institute of Educational Planning and Administration, Central Institute of Education;
History	–	Indian Council of Historical Research, National Archives of India, Nehru Memorial Museum and Library;
Labour	–	Indian Labour Institute;
Mass Communication	–	Indian Institute of Mass Communication;
Public Administration	–	Indian Institute of Public Administration;
Sociology	–	Delhi School of Social Work.

Delhi Public Library, as deposit centre under law, can play a great supporting role along with universities and IIT libraries. For particular form of literature, NASSDOC can be a resource centre for PhD. theses, research project reports, and working papers and ILRC for serials. It can be safely assumed that these libraries, among themselves, can fulfil at about 70 per cent needs of the scholars in Delhi. For the balance, other national resource centres in the country and outside can be contacted.

Pre-requisites

1. Government support and encouragement including formulation of a policy;
2. Adequate manpower and financial resources;
3. Computer and communication capabilities;
4. Reprographic facilities;
5. Permanent organisation to ensure delivery of service;
6. Compilation of location tools like Union Catalogues;
7. Storage/Depository facilities for preserving materials less

used in the libraries but important for research;
8. Carrier service to supply documents; and
9. Coordinated acquisition policy to aim at availability of at least one copy of every worthwhile national publication in social sciences in the cooperative network.

SYSTEM DESIGN

The organisational structure of INDOCSIS would consist of: (1) Central Loan Library, (2) Specialised Material Delivery Centres, and (3) Discipline-Oriented Centres. The system would be controlled by an Executive Committee and an Administrative Body with a small secretariat. Both of these will have members representing libraries and ministries/departments of Government of India.

Executive Committee

Its functions would be:

1. Formulation of a policy;
2. Formulation of plan of action;
3. Identifying bottlenecks and to take remedial measures;
4. Arranging necessary finances; and
5. Maintaining liaison with government departments like Communications, Transport, and Post and Telegraph for quick delivery of documents.

Administrative Committee

Its role would be:

(i) To lay down rules for lending;
(ii) To identify libraries for assigning responsibility of supplying documents within specific disciplines and to strengthen their resources accordingly;
(iii) To fix charges for the service which may include microfilming, photo-copying and documents delivery;
(iv) To monitor the services from time to time and take corrective steps; and(
(v) To frame rules for compiling Union Catalogues.

Central Loan Library

The Functions of this library would be:

(i) To coordinate the acquisition activities of other libraries vis-a-vis document supply service;
(ii) To identify gaps in the overall collection and take necessary steps accordingly;
(iii) To compile and keep updated Union Catalogues, preferably through computer;
(iv) To create translation facilities for foreign and Indian regional language documents;
(v) To provide micro-filming and reprographic facilities;
(vi) To provide online access to computerised Union Catalogue data through terminals;
(vii) To keep contact with national and international document delivery centres;
(viii) To conduct surveys and to sponsor seminars for improving the system;
(ix) To acquire bibliographical tools to verify references for document supply; and
(x) To act as central point for interaction between the participating libraries

Specialised Material Delivery Centres

Some libraries may be assigned responsibility to collect documents of special categories such as theses, research project reports, working papers, newspapers, government documents, etc.

Discipline-Oriented Libraries

These libraries would form the nucleus for document supply service in their disciplines and would shoulder major responsibility for its successful working.

WORKING INFRASTRUCTURE

We have a good number of document resource centres in Delhi and when properly coordinated in INDOCSIS, with resource material duly identified, these centres can provide a reasonable standard of service in document supply. For developing INDOCSIS, the resources of the existing Resource Centres will have to be strengthened and new Resource Centres developed where necessary.

Secretariat

The Secretariat of the Executive and Administrative Committees may be set-up in the Indian Council of Social Science Research (ICSSR). ICSSR is working at the national level for development of social science research and has taken up initiatives to support and develop a research information infrastructure.

Central Loan Library

NASSDOC Library can act as Central Loan Library. Its resource material will have to be developed on cooperative acquisition concept. It will avoid duplication and fill up gaps where found. NASSDOC has good reprographic facilities and is already successfully providing photocopies of the documents to research scholars in India and abroad.

Specialised Material Delivery Centres

NASSDOC may be identified to develop specialised collections of PhD. theses, Research Project Reports and Working Papers.

Theses Collection

NASSDOC has already a running programme of acquiring, on a token payment of Rs. 400 to the scholars, (1) PhD. theses approved by Indian Universities, and (2) foreign theses on India. It has so far acquired 3000 PhD. theses.

Research Project Reports Collection

ICSSR provides finances to Research Institutes and social scientists to conduct research in their fields. Consequently, copies of the reports of aided research projects are received by NASSDOC as contractual obligation. It has, at present, a collection of about 2000

Project Reports. With additional manpower, it can collect reports from other research centres in India. This material is particularly useful to administrators and planners in India since it is relevant to the socio-economic development plans.

Working Papers Collection

NASSDOC started building up a collection of working papers, which are useful as information source. This programme need to be stepped up.

Government Documents Collection

Central Secretariat Library (CSL) is a depository centre for government documents. It is open to government employees as well to general public. Supported by resource material in Parliament Library and other departmental libraries, it can provide efficient service in Government Documents supply. Compilation of Union Catalogue of Government Documents is, however, the foremost priority.

Periodical Literature

ILRC succeeded in collecting 100,000 volumes of periodicals supplied by about 38 libraries in Delhi as deposit or gratis. It subscribes to most of the Indian Social Science research periodicals and a selective number of foreign periodicals. If the present resources are further strengthened, it can provide document supply service in periodical literature on the lines of BLLD. *Union Catalogue of Periodicals*, an essential element for the service, has already been compiled, and with computerisation has to be kept updated.

Newspaper Collection

National Archives of India (NAI) and Nehru Memorial Museum and Library (NMML) have a good collection of back files of old and new newspapers in hard copy and microform. NMML has brought out a catalogue of newspapers available in microform. NASSDOC has also compiled a Union Catalogue of newspapers which records availability of 252 newspapers in 36 libraries and newspaper offices.

Discipline-Oriented Libraries

Libraries rich in literature in specific disciplines can take up responsibility for supplying the documents in original or its photocopy within its specialised area. For this, it has to be backed up by holdings of related discipline-oriented libraries. They will fill the gaps where necessary and build up a core collection to meet their information needs. The resource material in such libraries as the Institute of Economic Growth, Indian Institute of Public Administration, Institute of Applied Research Manpower, National Council of Educational Research and Training, Rattan Tata Library, etc., will require to be further strengthened. Funds will have to be provided for additional manpower and equipment.

Document Delivery

Rapid photo-copying facilities including facilities for making copies and enlarging microforms are an essential feature of any Document Supply System. Developments in information technology and communication system have now made it possible to achieve this and to deliver the same to the seeker/user in minimum time. Developed countries are now making use of electronic delivery systems. In India, at present, one cannot think of adopting such highly developed technology for this purpose. However, the minimum equipment required for the system would consist of carrier vans, telex and computer system (for central loan library only), telephones, photocopiers, microfilm/microficshe reader-cum-printer and computer terminals for participating libraries. In the long run, new technology could be gradually introduced to provide a faster service while taking into consideration the user requirements for speed and his/her willingness to bear the cost.

Network Members

Successful inter-library lending depends on ready cooperation between libraries. Networks for this activity should restrict the number at first to libraries which have major collections and are willing to participate. Therefore, to begin with, 30 libraries in Delhi may be selected for the network. The holding data of these selected libraries, fully computerised at the Central Loan Library, will help in locating the desired document. Besides mutual contact, the Central Node will have to coordinate delivery schedules through its own carrier service. Efforts may be made to allow members of one library to avail loan facilities in other libraries in the Network. This will reduce burden on inter-library loan system. After evaluating its working, more libraries may be allowed to join.

Barriers in Programme Operation

1. Copyright laws;
2. Restrictive condition on providing a certain category of material on loan to others;
3. Greater burden on some selective libraries which may deter them to part with their material;
4. Weak resource collection of libraries;
5. Lack of sufficient manpower resources resulting in delay in locating and retrieving material speedily;
6. Lack of proper equipment; and
7. Attitude of professional staff who tend to consider interlending an extra and unnecessary burden.

Monitoring and Evaluation of the System

The following points may be taken into consideration while evaluating the performance:

1. Documents must be available;
2. Requests must be transmitted quickly;
3. Documents must be transmitted quickly;
4. Accounting must be simple;
5. Procedure and forms must be simple and standardised;
6. System in the long run should be self-supporting;
7. Running cost per document supply should be minimum; and
8. It should contribute to the maximum to Universal Availability of Publications programmes/projects.

Conclusion

No matter how elegant an information system one may devise, its most important function will always be getting the information to the seeker/user. Document delivery is thus of prime importance.

To justify our professional existence, immediate concrete steps are needed towards setting up a suitable administrative structure with an appropriate fiscal foundation. A permanent organisation to ensure delivery of service is essential. Library cooperation is a difficult undertaking and, "requires a certain type of leadership, which can get results by persuasion and example rather than by demand and fiat. It requires careful participatory planning by those it will effect. It requires patience, understanding and faith on the part of administrators and legislators". (Evans, 1974). Professional organisations at national and regional level such as AGLIS, DLA, ILA, IASLIC and also professionals in the field will also have to face patiently the difficulties involved in the venture. Union Catalogues in the missing areas will have to be compiled. Catalogues already compiled will require to be kept updated. We may start with manual procedures, but aim at the complete mechanisation in the long run. The professionals' attitude and involvement will, however, play a decisive role in the success of the experiment.

BACKGROUNDERS

Anon, 1985, National Planning and the Impact of Electronic Technology on Document Provision and Supply, *Libri*, 35(3), p181-190.

Evans, Glyn T., 1974, Delivery Service, *In*: Kent, Allen, ed., 1974, *Resource Sharing in Libraries*, Marcel Deckker, New York, p120-136.

Landwehrmeyer, R., 1981, A Planned Decentralised Solution for National Document Supply : The Federal Republic of Germany, *Interlanding Review*, 9(9), p122-127.

Line, M.B., 1977, Universal Availability of Publications, *Unesco Bulletin for Libraries*, 31(3), p 142-151.

Nagarajan, K.S., 1966, Workflow in a Document Supply Service, *In:* Anon, 1966, *Papers : Seminar on Workflow in Special Libraries, University Libraries and Government Libraries, November 21-24, 1966, Delhi*, Indian National Scientific Documentation Centre, New Delhi, 10 p., Paper S-25.

Nitecki, Danuta, 1984, Document Delivery and the Rise of Automated Midwife, *Resource Sharing and Information Networks*, 1(3-4), p 83-101.

Reintges, J. Francis, 1984, Application of Modern Technologies to Inter-Library Resources Sharing Networks, *American Society for Information Science Journal*, 35(1), p 45-52.

Reynolds, Dennis J., 1980, Regional Alternatives for Inter-Library Loan : Access to Unreported Holdings, *College and Research Libraries*, 41(1), p 33-42.

Vervliet, H.D.L., 1981, Speaking for Cindrella : Unplanned Decentralised Interlending, *Interlending Review*, 9(4), p 28-30.

———, ed., 1979, *Resource Sharing of Libraries in Developing Countries*, K.G. Saur, New York, 280 p., IFLA Publication, 14.

Vickers, Stephen and Line, M.B., 1984, *Improving the Availability of Publications : A Comparative Assessment of Model National Systems*, International Federation of Library Associations and Institutions, International Programme for UAP, Boston Spa.

APPENDICES

APPENDIX-I

Social Science Research Institutions in India (Discipline-wise Selective List)

Agriculture
- Indian Agriculture Research Institute, New Delhi
- Indian Council of Agricultural Research, New Delhi
- Indian Society of Agricultural Economics, Bombay

Anthropology
- Anthropological Survey of India, Calcutta
- Madhya Pradesh Tribal Research and Development Institute, Bhopal
- Tribal Cultural Research and Training Institute, Hyderabad

Archaeology/Archives
- Archaeological Survey of India, New Delhi
- National Archives of India, New Delhi

Cooperation
- National Cooperative Development Corporation, New Delhi
- National Cooperative Union of India, New Delhi
- National Institute of Public Cooperation and Child Development, New Delhi
- Vaikunth Mehta National Institute of Cooperative Management, Pune.

Demography
- International Institute of Population Studies, Bombay

Education
- Directorate of Adult Education, New Delhi
- Indian Institute of Education, Pune
- National Council of Educational Research and Training, New Delhi
- National Institute of Educational Planning and Administration, New Delhi
- Raja Ram Mohan Roy National Educational Resources Centre, New Delhi

Foreign Trade and Investments
- Indian Investment Centre, New Delhi
- Indian Council for Research on International Economic Relations, New Delhi
- Institute of Foreign Trade, New Delhi

Geography
- National Geographical Society of India, Varanasi

History/Indology
- Asiatic Society of Bengal, Calcutta
- Asiatic Society of Bombay, Bombay
- Bhandarkar Oriental Research Institute, Pune
- Government Oriental Manuscript Library, Madras
- Heras Institute of Indian History and Culture, Bombay
- Indian Council of Historical Research, New Delhi

Khuda Baksh Oriental Public Library, Patna
Nehru Memorial Museum and Library, New Delhi
Raza Library, Rampur

Human Resources

Centre for Human Development and Social Change, Madras
Centre for Women Development Studies, New Delhi
Indian Council of Child Welfare, New Delhi
Institute for Applied Manpower Research, New Delhi
Labour Bureau, Shimla
Labour Document and Reference Centre, New Delhi
National Labour Institute, New Delhi
Sri Ram Centre for Industrial Relations and Human Resources, New Delhi
Xavier Labour Relations Institute, Jamshedpur

Industries

Centre for Research in Rural and Industrial Development, Chandigarh
Centre for Studies in Decentralised Industries, Bombay
Institute for Studies in Industrial Development, New Delhi
Small Industries Extension Training Institute, Hyderabad

Law

Indian Law Institute, New Delhi

Linguistics

Central Institute of Indian Languages, Mysore
Government Central Pedagogical Institute, Allahabad

Management

All India Management Association, New Delhi
Indian Institute of Management, Ahmedabad
Indian Institute of Management, Bangalore
Indian Institute of Management, Calcutta
Indian Institute of Management, Lucknow
Management Development Institute, Gurgaon
Motilal Nehru Institute of Research and Business Administration, Allahabad
National Institute of Bank Management, Bombay

Mass Communication

Indian Institute of Mass Communication, New Delhi

Political Science

Gokhale Institute of Politics and Economics, Pune
Gokhale Institute of Public Affairs, Bangalore
Indian Council of World Affairs, New Delhi
Institute of Constitutional and Parliamentary Studies, New Delhi
Institute of Defence Studies and Analysis, New Delhi

Psychology

B.M. Institute of Mental Health, Ahmedabad
Behavioural Science Centre, New Delhi
National Institute of Mental Health and Neuro-Sciences, Bangalore

Public Administration

Administrative Staff College of India, Hyderabad
Administrative Training Institute, Mysore
HCM State Institute of Public Administration, Jaipur

Indian Institute of Public Administration, New Delhi

Public Enterprises

Institute of Public Enterprises, Hyderabad

Bureau of Public Enterprises, New Delhi

Social Sciences (Comprehensive)

Centre for Studies in Social Sciences, Calcutta

GB Pant Social Science Institute, Allahabad

Indian Council of Social Science Research, New Delhi

Indian Institute of Advanced Study, Shimla

Indian School of Social Sciences, Trivandrum

National Social Science Documentation Centre, New Delhi

Tata Institute of Social Science, Bombay

Socio-Economic Development

AN Sinha Institute of Social Studies, Patna

Centre for Development Studies, Bhubaneshwar

Centre for Development Studies, Trivandrum

Centre for Economic and Social Studies, Hyderabad

Centre for Policy Research, New Delhi

Centre for Regional, Ecological and Science Studies in Development Alternatives, Calcutta

Centre for Rural Development, Hyderabad

Centre for Social Studies, Surat

Centre for the Study of Developing Societies, Delhi

Council for Social Development, New Delhi

Delhi School of Economics, Delhi

Delhi School of Social Work, Delhi

Gandhian Institute of Studies, Varanasi

Giri Institute of Development Studies, Lucknow

Gujarat Institute of Area Planning, Ahmedabad

Indian Institute of Economics, Hyderabad

Indian Social Institute, New Delhi

Institute of Development Studies, Jaipur

Institute of Economic Growth, Delhi

Institute for Social and Economic Change, Bangalore

LN Mishra Institute of Economic Development and Social Change, Patna

Madras Institute of Development Studies, Madras

National Council of Applied Economic Research, New Delhi

National Institute of Health and Family Welfare, New Delhi

National Institute of Public Finance and Policy, New Delhi

National Institute of Rural Development, Hyderabad

National Institute of Social Defence, New Delhi

National Institute of Urban Affairs, New Delhi

National Productivity Counicl, New Delhi

Sardar Patel Institute of Economic and Social Research, Ahmedabad

Vidya Bhawan Rural Institute, Udaipur

Xavier Institute of Social Service, Ranchi

Statistics

Census Operations, Madras

Central Statistical Organisation, New Delhi
Indian Statistical Institute, Calcutta
Indian Statistical Institute, New Delhi

Town and Country Planning

School of Planning and Architecture, New Delhi
Town and Country Planning Organisation, New Delhi

APPENDIX-II

Specialised Centres

Centre for Development and Instructional Technology, New Delhi

Established 1972. Specialises in development and communication technology subjects. Holds 3,700 books, 1237 microfilms, 10,000 product literature and data bases on magnetic tapes. Is input centre for documents produced in India for DEVSIS data base. Has ISIS package.

Centre for Rural Documentation, Hyderabad

Established 1958. Holds 60,000 books and bound periodicals, 10,000 reports. The indexing slant is towards policy-making

Centre for Women's Development Studies, New Delhi

Established 1980. Holds 5000 books, 3500 unpublished mimeo papers and reprints, 100 periodical subscriptions. Associated with Information Network for Women and Development Studies.

Consumer Education and Resource Centre, Ahmedabad

Established 1978. Holds 6000 books, 140 periodical subscriptions. Has an EIKO PC/XT (IBM PC Compatible) with Winchester Drive of 360 KB. Associated with Consumer Information Resource Centre.

Documentation Research and Training Centre, Bangalore

Established 1962. Activities include (1) Research programme, (2) Advisory Service, (3) Extension programme, (4) Training programme, and (5) Continuous Education programme.

Gokhale Institute of Politics and Economic, Pune

Established 1930. Specialises in the disciplines of Economics, Political Science, Sociology and Statistics. Holds 200,000 books, 1000 microforms. Depository centre for UN publications. Special collection includes British Parliamentary papers, Government documents of USA and Commonwealth countries.

Indian Council of World Affairs, New Delhi

Established 1944. Specialises in the disciplines of Economics, International Affairs and International Law. Holds 110,000 books and 11,500 microforms. Special collection includes press-clippings.

Indian Institute of Foreign Trade, New Delhi

Established 1964. Specialises in Trade literature. Holds 50,000 books and 5,000 UN documents

Indian Institute of Mass Communication, New Delhi

Established 1965. Holds 19,000 books, 180 periodical and 50 newspaper subscriptions. Created data base of all documents received in the library. Data base developed at H.P./3000 computer system using MINISIS software.

Indian Institute of Public Administration, New Delhi

Established 1954. Holds 1,55,000 publications, 500 periodicals subscription.

Indian Statistical Institute, Calcutta

Established 1931. Specialises in Computer Science, Economics and Statistics, etc. Holds 200,000 books and periodicals, 375,000 maps and 3,500 microforms.

Institute of Applied Manpower Research, New Delhi

Established 1962. Specialises in Economics, Management, Manpower and Statistics. Holds 14,000 books and 15,000 bound periodicals.

Institute of Defence Studies and Analysis, New Delhi.

Established 1965. Specialises in press clipping files on defence matters from approximate 35 dailies.

Institute of Public Enterprises, Hyderabad

Established 1964. Specialises in Management, Policy Studies and Public Enterprises Studies. Special collection includes annual reports of State and Central Government, Public Undertakings.

National Council of Applied Economic Research, New Delhi

Established 1956. Specialises in Agricultural Economics, Energy and Transportation. Holds 18,147 books, 20,938 reports, and 1,053 microforms. Has MINISIS software package and H.P/3000 computer.

National Council of Educational Research and Training, New Delhi

Established 1961. Holds 1,40,000 books, 400 periodical subscriptions.

National Documentation Centre on Mass Communication, New Delhi

Established 1976. Holds 31,000 documents, 90 serial publication. Special Collection includes 400 items in Central Information file.

National Documentation Centre for Health, Population and Family Welfare, New Delhi

Established 1977. Holds 55,500 publications, 11,000 press clippings. Has, IBM Compatible PC with 640 KRAM and 20 MIZ HDD, 132 Column Dot Matrix Printer.

National Informatics Centre, New Delhi

Established 1977. Specialises in developing interactive data bases in network of computers for Government of India and State Governments. Has undertaken development of the bibliographic system on techno-economic information documents. Developed Pilot System for the National Medical Library for providing medical retrieval services and that for the Ministry of Law, Justice and Company Affairs for Legal Information Retrieval System. Provides on-line bibliographies service for (i) Documents in the library, and (ii) News-items on electronics and computers. Uses MINISIS Application Package.

National Institute of Educational Planning and Administration, New Delhi

Established 1962. Specialises in developing training programmes for key level educational planners and administrators, and undertaking research of applied nature. Holds 42,000 books, 325 journal subscriptions. Special collection includes 150 subject files of newspaper clippings, also films, video and, audio cassettes, microfilms. Library provides computerised awareness service. Has CDS/ISIS Software package.

National Institute for the Mentally Handicapped, Hyderabad

Established 1984. Holds 2400 books, 300 reprints, 100 video and Audio Cassettes.

Nehru Memorial Museum and Library, New Delhi

Established 1964. Created special collections — Gandhiana, Nehruana, Indirana. Has 4,668 files of newspapers in English, Hindi and regional languages.

Parliament Library, New Delhi

Established 1921. Holds 500,000 monographs consisting of Central, State and Foreign Government reports, UN and allied agencies publications, gazettes, debates, rules, Acts, etc.

Planning Commission, New Delhi

Established 1950. Holds 150,000 books. Special collection consists of 5,000 pamphlets, 10,000 plans and 1000 maps.

Regional Information Centre for Development Policy Modelling, Pune

Established 1984. Sponsored by IRDC, Canada. Specialises in economic modelling to help policy-makers to choose a suitable model. Holds 2000 documents.

Research and Information System for the Non-Aligned and Other Developing Countries, New Delhi

Established 1984. Priority research areas are:

(i) Wage and payment problems of the developing countries,
(ii) Money and finance issues, and
(iii) Analytical digest of current trends in the world economy.

Research Centre for Womens Studies, SNDT Women's University, Bombay

Established 1974. Holds 2450 books, 59 periodical subscription. Future programmes include pressing into service IBM PC/AT WIPRO model minicomputer and CDS/ISIS software package.

Small Enterprises National Documentation Centre, Hyderabad

Established 1970. Provides comprehensive, economic, financial and technical information services to small industries. Holds 5,000 produce profiles and 5,000 trade catalogues.

Tata Institute of Social Science, Bombay

Established 1930. Specialises in personal management, rural and urban development and social work. Holds 58,000 books, 2000 pamphlets and 500 reprints.

APPENDIX-III

Documentation Resources

Abstracts of Books, Reports and Articles (Quarterly), Parliament Library, New Delhi

Accessions List : South Asia (Monthly), Library of Congress Office, Delhi.

Acquisition Up-date (Monthly), NASSDOC, New Delhi.

Agriculture Land Rural Development Abstracts (Irregular), Institute of Social and Economic Change, Bangalore.

Annotated Bibliography on the Economic History of India, 1500-1947, Gokhale Institute of Politics and Economics, Pune; Indian Council of Social Science Research, New Delhi.

Annual Bibliography of Banking Literature (Annual), National Institute of Bank Management, Bombay.

Appropriate Technology Documentation Bulletin (Monthly), Small Enterprises National Documentation Centre, Hyderabad.

Area Guides on China and Pakistan (Irregular), Institute of Defence Studies and Analysis, New Delhi.

Arth Suchi: Index of Indian Economic Literature (Quarterly), National Council of Applied Economic Research, New Delhi.
Computerised. Covers Development Literature of India.

Asian Social Science Bibliography (Adhoc), Institute of Economic Growth, Delhi. Since suspended.

Bibliographic Reprints (Quarterly), NASSDOC, New Delhi.

Bibliographies on Tap (Irregular), NASSDOC, New Delhi.

Bulletin of Documentation in Urban and Regional Planning (Quarterly), Town and Country Planning Organisation, New Delhi.

Bulletin on Film (Quarterly), National Documentation Centre on Mass Communication, New Delhi.

CORD Abstracts (Bi-Monthly), Centre for Rural Development, Hyderabad.

CORD Index (Monthly), Central for Rural Development, Hyderabad.

Chetna (Quarterly), National Medical Library, New Delhi.
Covers health literature; also includes information about new Indian Journals, MEDLARS Searches, Print outs, etc.

Clipping Services Bulletin (Bi-Monthly), Lalbhai Group of Rural Development, Ahmedabad.

Conference Alert (Quarterly), NASSDOC, New Delhi.

Current Articles of Interest (Monthly), Institute of Defence Studies and Analysis, New Delhi.

Current Awareness Service (Monthly), Indian Institute of Mass Communication, New Delhi.

Current Awareness Service (Monthly), National Documentation Centre on Mass Communication, New Delhi.

Current Contents (Bi-Monthly), Ministry of Labour, New Delhi.

Current Literature on Science of Science (Monthly), National Institute of Science Technology and Development Studies, New Delhi.

Current Management Literature (Monthly), Administrative Staff College of India, Hyderabad.

Current Management Literature (Quarterly), Indian Institute of Management, Ahmedabad.

Current News Weekly (Weekly), National Institute of Bank Management, Bombay.

Current Press Clipping Titles (Bi-Monthly), Indian Institute of Management, Bangalore.

Data India (Weekly), Press Institute of India, New Delhi.

Development and Welfare (Quarterly), Delhi School of Social Work, Delhi. Index of books with emphasis on developing countries.

DEVINDEX India, Centre for Development and Instructional Technology, New Delhi.

Digest of Legislative and Constitutional Cases, Parliament Library, New Delhi.

DOC-NIPCCD (Monthly), National Institute of Public Co-operation and Child Development, New Delhi.

DOC-PLAN (Quarterly), Planning Commission, New Delhi.

DOC-STAT (Quarterly), Central Statistical Organisation, New Delhi.

Documentation Bulletin (Quarterly), Centre for Studies in Decentralised Industries, Bombay.

Documentation Bulletin (Quarterly), Vaikunthabhai Mehta Smarak Trust, Bombay.

Documentation in Public Administration (Monthly), Indian Institute of Public Administration, New Delhi.

Documentation in Social Sciences (Bi-Monthly), ICSSR Southern Regional Centre, Hyderabad.

Documentation in Urban and Regional Planning Bulletin (Quarterly), Town and Country Planning Organisation, New Delhi.

Documentation Indian National Affairs (Quarterly), Chandigarh.

Documentation List (Monthly), Centre for Studies in Social Science, Calcutta.

Documentation List (Monthly), Tata Institute of Social Sciences, Bombay.

Documentation List: Society, Education and Islam (Annual), Jamia Millia Islamia, New Delhi.

Documentation of Foreign Trade (Monthly), Indian Institute of Foreign Trade, New Delhi.

Documentation of Public Administration (Monthly), Indian Institute of Public Administration, New Delhi.

Documentation on Asia (Annual), Indian Council of World Affairs, New Delhi. Since suspended.

Forthcoming Training Programmes/Seminars/Workshops (Occasional), Management Development Institute, Gurgaon.

Fortnightly List of Articles on India, Servants of India Society and Gokhale Institute of Politics and Economics, Pune.

Guide to Indian Periodical Literature (Quarterly), Indian Documentation Service, Gurgaon.

ICSSR Journal of Abstract and Reviews: . . . Indian Council of Social Science Research, New Delhi
. . . Economics (Quarterly)
. . . Geography (Half Yearly)
. . . Political Science (Half Yearly)
. . . Sociology and Social Anthropology (Half Yearly)

ICSSR Research Abstracts Quarterly, Indian Council of Social Science Research, New Delhi.

Index India (Quarterly), Rajasthan University, Jaipur.

Index of Articles relating to Agricultural Economics (Irregular), Indian Society of Agricultural Economics, Bombay. Computerised.

Index of Literature of Productivity and Management (Bi-Monthly), National Productivity Council, New Delhi.

Index of Periodicals Articles on Industrial Relations in India (Monthly), Sri Ram Centre for Industrial Relations and Human Resources, New Delhi.
Also included in *Indian Journal of Industrial Relations*

Index to Indian Economic Journals (Monthly), Calcutta.

Index to Indian Legal Periodicals, Indian Law Institute, New Delhi.

Indian Books: Annotated (Quarterly), Indian Council of World Affairs, New Delhi. Since suspended.

Indian Diary of Events (Quarterly), NASSDOC, New Delhi.

Indian Dissertation Abstracts (Quarterly), Indian Council of Social Science Research, New Delhi.

Indian Education Abstracts (Quarterly), Ministry of Human Resource Development, Department of Education, New Delhi. Since suspended.

Indian Press Index (Monthly), Delhi Library Association, Delhi.

Indian Psychological Abstracts (Quarterly), Indian Council of Social Science Research, New Delhi.

Kesari Shatabdi Suchi (Marathi), Kesari, Pune. Period included is 1881-1920.

Library Bulletin (Monthly), Centre for Studies in Social Science, Calcutta.

Library Bulletin (Quarterly), International Institute of Population Studies, Bombay.

List of Additions, Gokhale Institute of Politics and Economics, Pune.

List of Additions (Bi-Monthly), Indian Statistical Institute, New Delhi.

List of Additions (Monthly), Institute of Applied Manpower Research, New Delhi.

List of Additions (Monthly), Institute of Public Enterprise, Hyderabad.

List of Parliamentary Reports (Occasional), Institute of Public Enterprises, Hyderabad.

List of Selected Articles from Kannada Newspapers and Journals (Half Yearly), ICSSR Southern Regional Centre, Hyderabad. (Kannada).

List of Selected Articles from Telugu Newspapers and Journals (Half Yearly), ICSSR Southern Regional Centre, Hyderabad. (Telugu).

List of Selected Articles from Urdu Newspapers and Journals (Half Yearly), ICSSR Southern Regional Centre, Hyderabad. (Urdu).

MAN DEV Documentation (Fortnightly), Management Development Institute, Gurgaon.

Management Abstracts (Quarterly), All India Management Association, New Delhi.

Manpower Documentation (Quarterly), Institute of Applied Manpower Research, New Delhi.

NASSDOC Dockets (Monthly), National Social Science Documentation Centre, New Delhi. Since suspended.

NEHUNERC Documentation Bulletin (Bi-Monthly), North-Eastern Hill University and ICSSR North Eastern Regional Centre, Shillong.

NIHFW Accession List (Quarterly), National Institute of Health and Family Welfare, New Delhi.

National Catalogue of University Level Text-Books (Quarterly), Raja Ram Mohan Roy National Educational Resource Centre, New Delhi.

New Additions in NRLC Library (Half Yearly), National Research Laboratory and Conservation of Cultural Property, Lucknow.

Paging Periodicals (Bi-Monthly), National Social Science Documentation Centre, New Delhi. Presently suspended.

Quarterly Documentation List (Quarterly), Indian Council of Child Welfare, New Delhi.

Recent Additions (Monthly), Indian Institute of Management, Bangalore.

Recent Additions to the Library (Monthly) Planning Commission, New Delhi.

Research Abstracts Quarterly (Quarterly), Indian Council of Social Science Research, New Delhi.

Retrospective Cumulative Index of Indian Social Science Periodicals, National Social Science Documentation Centre, New Delhi. In process.

SPA Abstracts (Monthly), School of Planning and Architecture, New Delhi.

Samajik Vigyan Samachar (Monthly), National Social Science Documentation Centre, New Delhi. (Hindi). Since suspended.

Selected Articles on Modern Indian History (Monthly), Nehru Memorial Museum and Library, New Delhi.

Selected Documentation in Higher Education (Quarterly), University Grants Commission, New Delhi.

Social Science Documentation List (Half Yearly), ICSSR Western Regional Centre, Bombay.

Social Science News (Monthly), National Social Science Documentation Centre, New Delhi. Since suspended.

Suchika (Monthly), Jawaharlal Nehru University, New Delhi.

Social Science Research Index (Occasional), National Social Science Documentation Centre, New Delhi. Presently suspended.

Times of India Index (Quarterly), Times of India Publication, Bombay. Since suspended.

Urban Documentation (Quarterly), National Institute of Urban Affairs, New Delhi.

Weekly Current News Up-date, National Informatics Centre, New Delhi.

Weekly List of Articles (Weekly), Indian Council of World Affairs, New Delhi. Presently suspended.

APPENDIX-IV

Bibliographical Coverage of Doctoral Dissertations

Abstracts of Dissertations in Social Sciences, by S.A.H. Haqqi, Sterling, New Delhi, 1979, 305p.

Abstracts of PhD. Thesis, Indian Institute of Technology, Madras, 1980, 1070p.
vol 2, Technology, Humanities and Social Sciences; covers only three titles in Social Sciences.

Abstracts of the Thesis Accepted for the Doctorate Degree of Banaras Hindu University, 1927-1965, Banaras Hindu University, Varanasi, 6 vols.

Abstracts of the Thesis for D.Sc. and PhD., 1983-1972, Andhra University, Waltaire, 1972, 405p.

American Dissertations on Foreign Education, by Walter Crosby Felis, Committee on International Relations, Washington, 1950.
India, No. 1823-2133, p 88-100

Annotated Bibliography of Theses and Dissertations on Asia, Accepted at Syracuse University, compiled by Donn V. Hart, Syracuse University, New York, 1964, 46p.

Bibliography of Doctoral Dissertations: Social Sciences and Humanities, Association of Indian University, New Delhi.
The Retrospect coverage is from 1857. Current theses are reported in *University News* — the monthly journal of the Association.

Bibliography of Doctoral Thesis in . . . Accepted by Indian Universities, 1930, Association of Indian University, New Delhi.
Annual with cumulation supplement. Title varies.

Bibliography of Research in Indological Studies Carried Out in Various Universities in India, by Baijnath Sharma, *Maru Bharati*, Vol. 2, No. 2, July 1963, p 235-38.

Bibliography of Thesis, Indian Agricultural Research Institute, New Delhi, 1970, 172p.
Covers 160 entries on Agricultural Economics, Rural Sociology and Rural Social Psychology.

Bulletin of Research Theses and Dissertations in the Union of India, National Archives of India, New Delhi.
No 1 published in January 1955. Irregular.
Four issues published covering the period up to 1966, Lists about 1670 titles which include theses in progress. Tiles varies slightly.

Catalogue of Theses and Dissertations, 1950-1969, University of Poona, Jaykar Library, Pune, 1971, 249p.

Catalogue of Theses and Dissertations Available in the University Central Library, University of Udaipur, Central Library, Udaipur, 1968.

Classified List of Theses, Indian Agricultural Research Institute, New Delhi, 1967.

Columbia University Master's Essays and Doctoral Dissertations on Asia, 1957-1959, Columbia University, East Asiatic Library, New York, 1957, 96p.

A Compendium of Research, 1951-1976, ed. by M. Chennaveeriah, et al, Karnataka University, Dharwar, 1976, 386p.

Directory of Research Work in History in the University of Madhya Pradesh, Published in *Journal of the Madhya Pradesh Itihas Parishad*, No. 5, 1967, p 175-85; No. 6, 1969, p 1-5.

Dissertations in Economics, 1921-1971: Abstracts of M.A. and PhD. Theses, University of Bombay, Department of Economics, Bombay, 1974, 656p.

Dissertations in the Social Sciences by Indian Doctoral Scholars, 1933-1963, by Jagan Nath Kaul, University Microfilms, Ann Arbor, 1955, Publication No 12598.

Doctoral Dissertations, Rajasthan University, Jaipur 1966, 316p.

Doctoral Dissertations and Master's Theses on Asia, 1694-1962, University of Chicago Library; Far Eastern Library, Chicago, 1962, 52p.
Includes 145 titles on India and Pakistan

Doctoral Dissertations in Anthropology, 1959-1978: Summaries of Theses, University of Delhi, Department of Anthropology, Delhi, 1981, 99p.

Doctoral Dissertations on South Asia, 1966-1970: An Annotated Bibliography Covering North America, Europe, Australia, by Frank J. Shulman, Centre for South and South-East Asian Studies, Ann Arboor, 1971, 228p.
Includes 1, 305 entries on India and Pakistan

Doctorates in Social Sciences Awarded by Indian University up to 1967, Inter-University Board of India, (*now* Association of Indian Universities), Indian Council of Social Science Research, New Delhi, 1971, 401p., Research Information Series,
vol. 1, 1971, 402p
vol. 2, no. 1, 1970, 88p
vol. 2, no. 2, 1970, 99p
vol. 2, no. 3, 1972, 116p

Documentation of Doctoral Theses in Ancient Indian History, Culture, and Archaeology in the Banaras Hindu University, 1930-1968, Banaras Hindu University, Varanasi, 1970, Documentation Series, 15.

Documentation of Doctoral Theses in Economics in Banaras Hindu University, 1943-1967, Banaras Hindu University, Varanasi, 1969, Documentation Series, 11.

Documentation of Doctoral Theses in Geography in Banaras Hindu University, Banaras Hindu University, Varanasi, 1968, 21p., Documentation Series, 2.

Documentation of Doctoral Theses in History in the Banaras Hindu University, Benaras Hindu University, Varanasi, 1970.

Economics, Commerce, Management: A Bibliography of Doctoral Dissertation Accepted by Indian Universities, 1857-1870, Inter-University Board of India, (*now* Association of Indian Universities), New Delhi, 1973, 155p.

Economic Investigation in India: A Bibliography of Research, by Girija Prasad Gupta, 3rd edn, Rama Prasad and Sons, Agra, 1966, 180 p.
Work for PhD. and D.Litt. in Commerce and Economics; Covers post-Independence period; 3rd edn, is reprint of Ist edn, plus supplement.

Educational Investigations in Indian Universities: A List of Theses and Dissertations Approved for Doctorate and Master's Degree in Education, National Council of Educational Research and Training, New Delhi.
1939-1961, 1966, 286p.
1962-1966, 1968, 304p.

Foreign Theses on India, Social Science Documentation Centre, New Delhi, 1972, cyclostyled.

Index to Post-Graduate and Doctoral Dissertations in Political Science in Banaras Hindu University, 1939-1968, Banaras Hindu University, Varanasi 1970, Documentation Series, 16.

Indian Dissertation Abstracts, Indian Council of Social Science Research, New Delhi. Quarterly.

Indian Dissertation Abstracts Index, vol 1-10, 1973-1981, National Social Science Documentation Centre, New Delhi, 1985, NASSDOC Research Information Series, 25.

JNU Dissertation Index, compiled by AR Sethi, Jawaharlal Nehru University Library, Documentation Section, New Delhi, 1975, 118p.

List of Doctoral Theses Accepted by Indian Universities, published in *University News*, No. 1, 1963 on wards, Monthly

List of Doctoral Theses in Industrial Relations Approved by the Indian Universities during 1960-1963, published in *Indian Journal of Industrial Relations*, 1 (2) October, 1965, p. 231-37

List of Thesis Accepted for the Award of PhD. Degrees during the Years 1960-1978, Sardar Patel University, Vallabh Vidyanagar, n.d., 39p.

List of Theses Approved for the B.Sc., Ph D., M.Sc. and M.A. Degree in the Aligarh Muslim University, Aligarh, 1920-1969, Maulana Azad Library, Aligarh Muslim University, Aligarh, 1969. x, 68p., Reference and Research Publications, No 1.

National Register of Doctoral Dissertations Accepted and in Progress in Social Science and Humanities in Indian Universities, Council for Oriental Research, Bhopal, 1979, 8 vols

Vol 1, Economics, Demography, Agricultural Economics and Econometrics 264p.

Vol 1-B, Agricultural Economics 56p.

Vol 2, Political Science, International Politics, Constitutional Studies and Public Administration, 102p.

Vol 3, Education and Education Psychology, 141p.

Vol 4, Sociology, Social Anthropology and Criminology

Vol 5, Commerce, Business Administration, Business Management, Labour, Personnel Administration, 280p.

Vol 6, History and Geography

Vol 7, Law and Criminology, 34p.

Vol 8, Psychology, 102p.

Punjab University Doctoral Dissertations 1948-1964, compiled by Ramesh C. Sharma and Raj Kumar Puri, edited by S.S. Lal, Punjab University, Extension Library, Ludhiana, 1965, 22p.

Supplement 1965-1967, 1968, 15p.

Main publication and Supplement contain 349 entries.

Research Abstracts, Maharaja Sayajirao University of Baroda, Faculty of Education and Psychology, Baroda, 1963, 40p.

Research in the Annamalai University, Annamalai University, Annamalai, 1955, 36p.

Research in Political Science in India: A Detailed Bibliography, by Brajendra Pratap Gautam, Oriental Publishing House, 1965.

South Asian History, 1750-1950: A Guide to Periodicals, Dissertations and Newspapers, by Margaret H. Case, London, 1968.

Dissertations, p 385-439.

Studies on Mass Communication in Asia, Asian Mass Communication Research and Information Centre, Singapore.

Synopsis of Doctoral Theses in Social Sciences, 1955-1975, Karnataka University, Dharwar, 1978, 365p.

Theses in Jawaharlal Nehru Library, Jawaharlal Nehru Library, Doctor Harisingh Gour University, Sagar, 1967, 72p.

Thesis in SSDC: A Bibliography, Social Science Documentation Centre, New Delhi, 1983, NASSDOC Research Information Series, 3.

Theses in Social Sciences in Punjab Agricultural University, Ludhiana, ICSSR North Western Regional Centre, Chandigarh.

Theses on Asia Accepted by Universities in United Kingdom and Ireland 1967-1964, compiled by B.C. Bloomfield, London, 1967, 127p.

Lists 2571 titles arranged by country with subject section.

Theses on Indian Sub-Continent, 1877-1971: An Annotated Bibliography of Dissertations in Social Sciences and Humanities Accepted with the Universities of Australia, Canada, Great Britain and Ireland, and United States of America, compiled by Krishna Gopal, edited by Dhanpat Rai, Hindustan Publishing Co., Delhi, 1977, 462p.

Covers 376 entries.

Titles of Theses and Dissertations Approved for the Doctorate and Master's Degree Deposited in the University Library, Mysore University Library, Mysore, 1961, 26p.

Universities News (Monthly), Association of Indian Universities, New Delhi

No 1, 1963 –

Includes *List of Doctoral Theses Accepted by Indian Universities*.

APPENDIX-IV A

Bibliographical Coverage of Doctoral Dissertations in Great Britain and USA: Brief Survey

GREAT BRITAIN

Index to Theses Accepted for Higher Degrees by the Universities of Great Britain and Ireland and the Council for National Academic Awards (Semi-Annual), ASLIB, London.

Retrospective Index to Theses of Great Britain and Ireland, 1716-1950, by R. Bilboul, Clio Press, Santa Barbara, California

UNITED STATES OF AMERICA

Comprehensive Dissertation Index, 1861-1972, University Microfilms, Ann Arbor, Michigan, 1973, 37 vols.
The CDI data base also offers computerised service DARIX II, and on request prepares cumulative inter-disciplinary listings of dissertations in any field.

Dissertation Abstracts International (Monthly), University Microfilms Inc., Ann Arbor, Michigan,

APPENDIX-V

ICSSR Surveys of Research in Social Science

Accounting Theory, Popular, Bombay, 1976, 94p.
Demography, Popular, Bombay, 1975, 440p.
Economics and Social History of India, Ajanta, New Delhi, 1986, 283p.
Economic, Allied, New Delhi
- vol. i. Methods and Techniques, 1977, 136p
- vol. ii. Macro Economic 1976, 424p.
- vol. iii. Agriculture I, 1975, 264p.
- vol. iv. Agriculture II, 1975, 345p.
- vol. v. Industry, 1975, 362p.
- vol. vi. Infrastructure, 1980, 292p.
- vol. vii. Econometrics, 1978, 395p.

Geography, Popular, Bombay 1972, 398p.
Geography, 1969-1972, Second Series, Allied, New Delhi, 1979, 234p.
Geography, 1972-1975, Third Series, Concept, New Delhi, 1984, 194p.
Geography, Physical, Concept, New Delhi, 1983, 332p.
Management, Vikas, New Delhi
- vol. i. 1973, 502p.
- vol. ii. 1977, 684p.

Political Science, Allied, New Delhi
- vol. i. Political System, 1979, 278p.
- vol. ii. Political Process, 1981, 232p.
- vol. iii. Political Dynamics, 1981, 170p.
- vol. iv. Political Thought, 1986, 288p.
- vol. v. International Studies 1988, 336p.

Psychology, Popular, Bombay, 1972, 454p.
Psychology, 1971-1976, Popular, Bombay
- Part-I, 1980, 371p.
- Part-II, 1981, 507p.

Psycholosy in India : The State of Art Sage, New Delhi
- vol. i. Personality and Mental Process, 1988, 357p
- vol. ii. Basic and Applied Social Psychology, 1988, 353p.
- vol. iii. Organisational Behaviour and Mental Health, 1988, 387p.

Public Administration, Allied, New Delhi
- vol. i. 1973, 352p.
- vol. ii. 1975, 556p.

Public Administration, 1970-1979, Second Series, New Delhi, Concept, 1986, 267p.
Sociology and Social Anthropology, Popular, Bombay
- vol. i. 1974, 479p.

vol. ii.	1974, 599p.
vol. iii.	1976, 336p.

Sociology and Social Anthropology, 1969-1979, Satvahan, New Delhi

vol. i.	1985, 264p.
vol. ii.	1985, 345p.
vol. iii.	1986, 265p.

APPENDIX-VI

Current Documentation Projects Receiving Financial Assistance

1. Annotated Bibliography of Research in Development Psychology
2. Annotated Bibliography on Health, Nutrition and Family Planning Programmes with special reference to Tribal Set-up
3. Annotated Bibliography of Kannada Reference Tools
4. Annotated Guide to Reference Sources in Telugu
5. Encyclopaedia of Social Sciences in Marathi
6. Index of Articles on Agricultural Economics
7. Information Requirements and Suggestions for Developing Library and Information Services for Social Scientists in India.
8. Union Catalogue of Rare Books in Social Sciences published in 16th Century and onwards
9. Union Catalogue of 18th and 19th Century Newspapers published or available in the State of Maharashtra

APPENDIX-VI A

Documentation Projects Earlier Sponsored

1. Association of Clinical Psychologists, Delhi
   Perceived Quality of Work, Life and Role Stress in Organisation: A Bibliographical Study
2. Association of Indian Universities, New Delhi
   Preparation of *Doctoral Awards by the Indian Universities in Social Sciences*
3. Behavioural Science Centre, New Delhi. *Studies in Communal Behaviour with Special Reference to Hindu-Muslim Tension: A Bibliographical Analysis*
4. Bangalore University, Department of Library Science, Bangalore
   Union Catalogue of reference tools in social science in Bangalore city libraries
5. Delhi Library Association, Delhi. *Bringing out of Indian Press Index* including its Book Review Supplement
6. Dharma Samaj College, Aligarh
   Socio-economic Implications of Puranic Legends: A Chronological Bibliographical Survey
7. Government of India Librarian's Association, New Delhi
   Preparation of *Directory of Government Department Libraries and Who's Who for the year 1983*
8. Indian Institute of Public Administration, New Delhi
   Study of the bibliographical control and distribution mechanism of State government publications and compilation of *Select Bibliography of State Government Publications*
9. Indian Society of Agricultural Economics, Bombay
   Index of Articles on Agricultural Economics
10. Indira Gandhi Open University, New Delhi
    Annotated Guide to References Sources in Telugu
11. Institute of Economic Growth, Delhi
    Preparation of *Asian Social Science Bibliography*
12. Institute of Peace Research & Actions, New Delhi
    Preparation of *Bibliography on Peace Studies Research*
13. Institute of Public Enterprises, Hyderabad
    Preparation of *Annotated Bibliography on Public Enterprises*
14. Institute for Studies in Social Sciences, Calcutta
    Project on Dawn of a Century 1900-1910: Socio-Political Documentation
15. Karnataka University, Department of Library Sciences, Dharwad
    Preparation of *Annotated Bibliography of Kannada Reference Sources in Social Sciences*
16. Lucknow University, Department of Library Science, Lucknow
    Compilation of *Union List of Periodicals in Social Sciences in Lucknow*

17. M.S. University of Baroda, Department of Child Development, Baroda.
Preparation of *Annotated Bibliography on Health, Nutrition and Family Planning Programmes with Special Reference to Tribal Set-up*
18. M.S. University of Baroda, Department of Child Development, Baroda
Preparation of *Annotated Bibliography of Research in Development Psychology, 1975-85*
19. Nagari Pracharini Sabha, New Delhi
Preparation of *Bibliography of Hindi Language Publications in Social Sciences*
20. Nagpur University, Department of Library & Information Sciences, Nagpur
Compilation of *Union Catalogue of Social Science Periodicals on Library and Information Science in Indian Universities*
21. National Conference on Child Education, Delhi
Compilation of *Who's Who of Children's Writing*
22. Rabindra Bharati University, Calcutta
Compilation of *Bibliography of M.N. Roy*
23. Rajasthan University, Department of History, Jaipur
Project on the *Study of Thikana Records*
24. Research Foundation, New Delhi
Preparation of *Bibliography on Socio-Cultural Life of the People of Arunachal Pradesh*
25. S.P. Agrawal and A. Biswas
Updating on *Indian Educational Documents since Independence: Committees, Commissions & Conferences*
26. Samaj Vidnayan Mandal, Pune
Preparation of *Encyclopaedia of Social Sciences in Marathi*
27. Socio-Economic Research Institute, Calcutta
Economic Writings in Bengali, 1880-1947
28. Tilak Swaraj Sangh, Lokmanya Tilak Smarak Trust, Pune
Compilation of *Union Catalogue of 18th and 19th Century Newspapers published or available in the State of Maharashtra*
29. United Service Institute of India, New Delhi
Compilation of *Union Catalogue of Rare Books in Social Sciences Published in 16th century and onwards*

APPENDIX-VII

NASSDOC Exchange Partners in Asia and the Pacific

Bangladesh
Association of Development Agencies in Bangladesh
Bangla Desh Institute of Development Studies
Centre of Integrated Rural Development for Asia and the Pacific
National Library of Bangladesh
Social Science Research Council

Bhutan
National Institute of Education

China People's Republic
Academy of Social Sciences
National Library of China

China Republic
Institute of International Relations
Resource and Information Centre for Chinese Studies

Hong Kong
Chinese University of Hong Kong
Social Research Centre

Indonesia
Centre for Strategic and International Studies
National Library of Indonesia
Perpustakan Museum Pusat

Iran
International Institute of Adult Literacy Methods

Iraq
Ministry of Culture and Information

Japan
Centre for East Asian Cultural Studies
Hitotsubashi University Library
Institute of Developing Economics
Japan Statistics Bureau
Japanese Psychological Association
Keio Economic Society
Research Institute for Economics and Business Administration

Korea (Federal Republic)
Institute of Economic Research
Korean Social Science Research Council
Research Institute of Asian Economics

Malaysia
Malaya University
Rubber Research Institute of Malaysia
UN Asian and Pacific Development Centre

Nepal
Research Centre for Nepal and Asian Studies
Tribhuvan University Economics Instruction Committee

New Zealand
Conterbury University Library
Massey University Library

Pakistan
Institute of Economic Studies
Pakistan Institute of Development Economics
Punjab University Library

Philippines

Philippines Social Science Council
Philippines University Asian Centre
Population Centre Foundation

Singapore

Asian Mass Communication Research and Information Centre
National Library

Sri Lanka

Centre for Development Information
Sri Lanka Centre for Development Studies

Thailand

National Institute of Development Administration
Unesco Regional Office for Education in Asia and the Pacific

APPENDIX-VIII

ICSSR Regional Centres

1. ICSSR Eastern Regional Centre
   10, Jadunath Sarkar Road
   Calcutta, West Bengal-700 029
   Phones: 466472; 467958
2. ICSSR North-Eastern Regional Centre
   NEHU Library Building, Mayurbhanj House
   Shillong-793 003
   Phone: 3941
3. ICSSR Northern Regional Centre
   Jawaharlal Nehru University
   New Delhi - 110 067
   Phone: 387343
4. ICSSR North-Western Regional Centre
   Punjab University Library Building
   Chandigarh - 160 014
   Phones: 25023; 29582
5. ICSSR Southern Regional Centre
   Osmania University Library
   Hyderabad, Andhra Pradesh-500 007
   Phone: 71756
6. ICSSR Western Regional Centre
   Vidya Nagari, Kalina, Bombay, Maharashtra - 400 098
   Phones: 554943; 532241

APPENDIX-IX

ILRC Participating Libraries

Central Secretariat Library
Shastri Bhavan
Dr. Rajendra Prasad Road
New Delhi-110001

Delhi Public Library
S.P. Mukerjee Marg
Delhi-110006

Delhi School of Social Work
University of Delhi
3, University Road
Delhi-110007

Department of Administrative Reforms
Cabinet Secretariat
Sardar Patel Bhavan
Parliament Street
New Delhi-110001

Directorate of Non-Formal (Adult) Education
West Block
8 Wing, 7 R.K. Puram
New Delhi-110022

Ford Foundation
55 Lodi Estate
New Delhi-110003

Indian Council of Cultural Relations
Azad Bhavan
Indraprastha Estate
New Delhi-110001

Indian Council of World Affairs
Sapru House, Barakhamba Road
New Delhi-110001

Institute of Defence Studies and Analyses
Sapru House, Barakhamba Road,
New Delhi-110001

Indian Institute of Public Administration
Indraprastha Estate
New Delhi-110001

Jawaharlal Nehru University
New Mehrauli Road
New Delhi-110065

MANAS
C/o Behavioural Sciences Centre
32 Netaji Subhash Marg
New Delhi-110002

Ministry of Finance
North Block
New Delhi-110001

Ministry of Home Affairs
North Block
New Delhi-110001

Ministry of Labour
Sharam Shakti Bhavan
Rafi Marg
New Delhi-110001

National Archives of India
Janpath
New Delhi-110001

Nehru Memorial Museum and Library
Teen Murti House
New Delhi-110011

National Council of Applied Economic Research
Parisila Bhavan, Indraprastha Estate
New Delhi-110001

National Social Science Documentation Centre
35 Ferozeshah Road
New Delhi-110001

Planning Commission Library
Yojana Bhavan
Parliament Street
New Delhi-110001

Prime Minister's Secretariat
South Block
New Delhi-110001

Ratan Tata Library
Delhi School of Economics
Delhi University
Delhi-110007

Registrar General of India
Kotah House
24 Mansingh Road
New Delhi-110001

United States Agency for International Development Mission to India
American Embassy, Chanakyapuri
New Delhi-110021

University Grants Commission
Bahadur Shah Zafar Marg
New Delhi-110001

APPENDIX-X

NASSDOC Research Information Series

1982

1. Union List of Social Science Periodicals Received in Delhi Libraries. Rev. in 1985.

1983

2. Union Catalogue of Newspapers: Delhi Libraries.
3. Theses in SSDC: A Bibliography.
4. Bibliography of Bibliographies in SSDC.
5. Research Project Reports in SSDC: A Bibliography.
6. Social Science Research Methodology: A Bibliography.
7. Bibliography of Bibliographies, compiled in SSDC.
8. Periodocals in SSDC: A Current List.
9. Reference Sources in SSDC: A Bibliography.

1984

10. Bibliography of Bibliographies: Supplement.
11. Recent India Books in Economics, Education, Political Science and Sociology.
12. Social Science Institutions and Organizations in India.
13. Andaman and Nicobar Islands: A Bibliography.
14. A Guide to Books & Journals Aided/Published by ICSSR.
15. Inter-Library Resources Centre: Holdings of Periodicals. Rev. ed.
16. Index of Seminars on North East (March 1975-April 1984) conducted by North-Eastern India Council of Social Science Research, Shillong.
17. ICSSR Research Abstracts Quarterly Index. Vol. I-II, 1971-1982.
18. Bibliography of Bibliographies, compiled in SSDC. Supplement 2.

1985

19. Inventory of Social Science Institutions and Organizations in India.
20. Documents in Microform: A List of Resources at SSDC, JNU, University of Bombay, ICSSR Regional Centre, Calcutta.
21. Library and Information Science Literature: SSDC Resource List.
22. Bibliography of Bibliographies: Supplement 3.
23. Periodicals in SSDC: A Current List.
24. Indian Dissertation Abstracts Index Vol. 1-10: 1973-1981.

25. Dr. S.R. Ranganathan: A Bibliography.
26. Distance Education: A Reading List.
27. Union List of Current Social Science Periodicals: Delhi Libraries.
28. National Integration: Literature in SSDC.
29. Bibliographic Reprints: Library Science and Informatics.
30. Family Welfare Education in India: A Bibliography.
31. Statistics and Data Sources: Part I: SSDC Resources.

1986

32. Bibliographic Reprints: Youth.
33. Recent Indian Books in Economics, Eduction, Political Science, Sociology and Social Anthropology.
34. Indian Social Science Periodicals: Survey, Part-I: Pre-Independence.
35. Mythic Society Library, Bangalore: Catalogue of Periodicals, 1985.
36. Social Science in the Present Day World.
37. Goa, Daman & Diu: A Preliminary List.
38. Union List of Social Science Periodicals: Lucknow.
39. Bibliography on Student Teaching.
40. Union Catalogue of Library Science and Informatics Publications: Delhi Libraries.
41. Bibliographic Reprints: Children.

1987

42. NASSDOC Source Book of Institutions: Part I.
43. Madhya Pradesh: A Select List.
44. Bibliographic Reprints: Women.
45. NASSDOC: How it works.
46. Thesauri, Glossaries, Terminologies Dictionaries in NASSDOC: A Resource Lost.
47. Recent Indian Books on Economics, Education, Political Science, Sociology, and Social and Cultural Anthropology, 1986.
48. Bibliographic Reprints: Tourism and Transportation.
49. Punjab, Haryana and Himachal Pradesh: A Select List.
50. Bibliographic Reprints: Labour and Labour Classes.
51. Bibliographic Reprints: Scheduled Caste and Scheduled Tribes.
52. Bibliographic Reprints: Social Problems (Drug Abuse, Family and Health, etc).
53. Bibliographic Reprints: Psychology.
54. Bibliographic Reprints: Economic Development.
55. Swatantrata Ke Paschat Bal Sahitya (Hindi)
56. Bibliographic Reprints: Banks and Banking.
57. Index to Indian Journals: Sociology and Psychology.
58. Bibliographic Reprints: Foreign Collaboration.
59. Periodicals in NASSDOC: 1987.
60. University of Delhi: Research in Library and Information Science: A Bibliographical Survey.

61. Bibliographic Reprints: Industry.
62. Bibliographic Reprints: Commerce.
63. Bibliographic Reprints: National Integration.

1988

64. Bibliography of Bibliographies.
65. Rajasthan: A Select List.
66. Directory of Exchange Service.
67. Bibliography Reprints: Management.
68. Recent Indian Books in Social Sciences.
69. Bibliographic Reprints Reports: Commerce.
70. Abstracts of Research Reports: Commerce.

1989

71. Public Finance : Bibliography, 2 vols.
72. Madhya Pradesh : Chayet Suchi.
73. Rajasthan : Chayet Suchi.
74. Bihar : Chayct Suchi.
75. Punjab, Haryana, Himachal Pradesh and Chandigarh : Chayet Suchi.
76. Uttarr Pradesh : Chayet Suchi.
77. Orissa : A Select List.
78. Karnataka : A Select List.
79. Delhi : Chayet Suchi.
80. West Bengal : A Select List.

NASSDOC Serials

1. Acquisition Update (Monthly).
2. APPINES Newsletter (Quarterly)
3. Bibliographies on Tap (Irregular)
4. Conference Alert (Quarterly).
5. Indian Diary of Events (Quarterly).
6. NASSDOC Dockets (Monthly)
7. Paging Periodicals (Bi-Monthly).
8. Samajik Vigyan Samachar (Monthly) (Hindi)
9. Social Science Research Index (Irregular)
10. Bibliographic Reprints.
11. Social Science News Index.

CICIL LIST

CONCEPTS IN COMMUNICATION, INFORMATICS & LIBRARIANSHIP

(CICIL)

General Editor: **S.P. AGRAWAL**

CICIL-1 Development of Library Services in India: Social Science Information
S.P. Agrawal Rs. 150

CICIL-2 Development of Documentation in India: Social Science Information
S.P. Agrawal Rs. 250

CICIL-3 UNESCO and Social Sciences: Retrospect and Prospect
S.P. Agrawal and J.C. Aggarwal Rs. 250

CICIL-4 INDIANA : A Bibliography of Bibliographical Sources
M.K. Jain Rs. 200

CICIL-5 Dimensions of Library and Information Science: Kaula Festschrift
V. Venkatappaiah (Eds.) Rs. 600

CICIL-6 Book Numbers: Some Indian Methods
M.P. Satija and S.P. Agrawal Rs. 100

CICIL-7 National Policy for University Libraries in India: Problems and Perspectives
N.B. Inamdar and L.S. Ramaiah (Ed.) Rs. 250

CICIL-8 Media Utilisation for the Development of Women and Children
B.S. Thakur and Binod C. Agrawal Rs. 150

CICIL-9 Terrorism: An Annotated Bibliography
Susheela Bhan (Ed.) Rs. 275

CICIL-10 Transnational Library Relations: The Indo-American Experience
M.B. Konnur Rs. 175

CICIL-11 Geography of Marketing and Commercial Activities in India
(Documentation on Research Information)
R.S. Dixit Rs. 130

CICIL-12 Information India 1988: Global View
S.P. Agrawal and **J.C. Aggarwal** Rs. 200

CICIL-13 Women's Education in India: Historical Review, Present Status and Perspective Plan
S.P. Agrawal and **J.C. Aggarwal** Rs. 360

CICIL-14 Cultural Communication in India: Role and Impact of Phonograms
J.M. Ojha (in press)

CICIL-15 Second Historical Survey of Educational Development in India: Select Documents 1985-1989
S.P. Agrawal and **J.C. Aggarwal** Rs. 490

CICIL-16 Documentation Encyclopaedia of UNESCO and Education
J.C. Aggarwal and **S.P. Agrawal** Rs. 800 (set of 2 parts)

CICIL-17 Attitude Towards Information: A Study of Post-Graduate Teachers and Researchers in Social Sciences
N.G. Satish (in press)

CICIL-18 Librarianship and Bureaucratic Organisation: A Study in the Sociology of Library Profession in India
P.K. Jayaswal Rs. 175

CICIL-19 Literature Search
K.A. Isaac Rs. 150

CICIL-20 Child Education in India: Index to Scholarly Writings in Indian Educational Journals and Newspapers since independence
S.P. Agrawal and **Naresh Kanta** Rs. 100

CICIL-21 Lok Sabha and Vidhan Sabha Elections in India 1989 & 1990: Process and Results with Comparative Study of Manifestos
S.P. Agrawal and **J.C. Aggarwal** Rs. 250

CICIL-22 Islamic Studies in India: A Survey of Human, Institutional and Documentary Sources
Mohamed Taher Rs. 180

CICIL-23 Panchayati Raj: An Annotated Bibliography
N.B. Inamdar, N.G. Satish and Anil Takalkar 290

CICIL-24 Information India 1989-90: Global View
S.P. Agrawal and J.C. Aggarwal Rs. 500

CICIL-25 First Handbook of Psychological and Social Instruments
Udai Pareek and T. Venkateswara Rao (in press)

CICIL-26 Educational and Social Uplift of Backward Classes: At What Cost and How? Mandal Commission and After
S.P. Agrawal and J.C. Aggarwal Rs. 275

CICIL-27 Mass Media and New Horizons: Impact of TV & Video an Urban Milieu
H.R. Trivedi Rs. 180

CICIL-28 Indian Writings on Education : An Indicator to Indian Educational Journals Grouped by Subject Deseriptors 1979 to 1986 (in two parts)
S.P. Agarwal Rs. 900 (per set)

CICIL-29 Nation in Crisis
S.P. Agrawal and J.C. Aggarwal Rs. 200

CICIL-30 Information India 1990-91: Global View
S.P. Agrawal and J.C. Aggarwal Rs. 500

CICIL-31 Development of University Libraries in India After Independence
O.P. Gupta Rs. 270

CICIL-32 Handbook on Child : With Historical Background
Pramila Pandit Barooah Rs. 320

CICIL-33 Weaker Section in Indian Society : Undiscovered Past, Uncertain Present and Unpredictable Future Index to Writings in Indian Scholarly Journals and 10 National Newspapers Classified under 1500 Descriptors 1886-1990
S.P. Agrawal and Rajeev Kumar Sharma Rs. 600

CICIL-34 Communication Informatics and Librarianship in India : An Introductory Guide to Publications Based on a Survey of Libraries in Capital of City India
S.P. Agrawal and Pushpa Rani Sharma Rs. 720

CICIL-35 Problems of Collection Development in Special Libraries
M.S. Sridhar Rs. 225

CICIL-36 National Information Resources for Social Sciences in India : Mobilisation, Dispersal and International Enhancement
S.P. Agrawal Rs 225